UNIVERSITY OF NORTH CAROLINA AT CHAPEL HILL
DEPARTMENT OF ROMANCE LANGUAGES

NORTH CAROLINA STUDIES
IN THE ROMANCE LANGUAGES AND LITERATURES

Founder: URBAN TIGNER HOLMES

Distributed by:

UNIVERSITY OF NORTH CAROLINA PRESS
CHAPEL HILL
North Carolina 27514
U.S.A.

NORTH CAROLINA STUDIES IN THE
ROMANCE LANGUAGES AND LITERATURES
Number 202

THE PERIPHRASTIC FUTURES FORMED
BY THE ROMANCE REFLEXES OF *VADO (AD)*
PLUS INFINITIVE

THE PERIPHRASTIC FUTURES FORMED BY THE ROMANCE REFLEXES OF *VADO (AD)* PLUS INFINITIVE

BY

JAMES JOSEPH CHAMPION

CHAPEL HILL

NORTH CAROLINA STUDIES IN THE ROMANCE
LANGUAGES AND LITERATURES
U.N.C. DEPARTMENT OF ROMANCE LANGUAGES

1978

Library of Congress Cataloging in Publication Data

Champion, James Joseph.
　　The periphrastic futures formed by the Romance reflexes of vado (ad) plus infinitive.

　　(North Carolina studies in the Romance languages and literatures; no. 202)
　　An earlier version was submitted as the author's thesis, University of Michigan, 1973.
　　Bibliography: p.
　　1. Latin language—Tense. 2. Romance languages—Tense. I. Title. II. Series.

PA2257.C5　　　　475　　　　78-16441
ISBN 0-8078-9202-5

I.S.B.N. 0-8078-202-5

DEPÓSITO LEGAL: V. 2.242 - 1978　　　I.S.B.N. 84-399-8747-1
ARTES GRÁFICAS SOLER, S. A. - JÁVEA, 28 - VALENCIA (8) - 1978

An earlier version of the present study was submitted and accepted as partial fulfillment of the requirements for the degree of Doctor of Philosophy in Romance Languages and Literatures: Romance Linguistics at the University of Michigan in December, 1973.

I should like to express my gratitude to Professor Ernst Pulgram for his critical guidance.

TABLE OF CONTENTS

	Page
Introduction	11
Chapter	
I. The Historical Emergence of Periphrases Formed by Romance Reflexes of "vado (ad)" plus Infinitive	21
II. The Stabilization of "vado (ad)" plus Infinitive	33
III. Extension of Usage and Grammatical Treatment of Periphrastic "vado (ad)" plus Infinitive	45
Appendix	66
Bibliography	
Works Cited	71
Abbreviations and Texts Cited	75

INTRODUCTION

The history of the expression of futurity from Proto-Indo-European through Latin to Romance has been one of fluctuation. A number of possibilities have always existed side by side. Indeed, it is safe to say that at no time was there only one way to express futurity. Obviously, some constructions have met with more success than others. Some never achieved popularity. Others may have become popular, only to be discarded later. Still others may have been restricted locally as spoken Latin began to be differentiated into what would become the Romance dialects.[1]

Proto-Indo-European most likely had no marked future paradigm: "The existence of a distinctive future tense... is doubtful. Future time might be expressed by the present indicative... by the subjunctive... or by certain -s- formations with desiderative and future force [e.g., Skt. *dāsyāmi*, Osc.-Umbr. *fust*]."[2] But if such a marked

---

[1] It is generally accepted among linguists that a distinction must be made between spoken and written Latin, and that the Romance dialects are a continuation of spoken Latin (some prefer to call it Proto-Romance). It is no longer seriously believed that the Romance dialects came about as a result of the progression Classical Latin > Vulgar Latin > Romance dialects. I shall here use the term "Latin" in its broadest sense, to refer to manifestations of spoken *and* written Latin from the time of the earliest records until we, rather arbitrarily, speak no longer of Latin, but of Romance. The List of Abbreviations contains the titles and editions of works from which I have taken examples, as well as the titles of works given in an abbreviated form in quotations. A word should be added here on spelling. In Latin, until the second century A.D., one letter was used to represent both vocalic [u] and consonantal [w]. In many modern editions of Latin works two letters are used: *u* for the former, and *v* for the latter. I shall follow this modern convention here, as, for example, in the title of this study. I shall not, however, alter the spelling in sources quoted.

[2] Buck 1933, 278.

future form *did* exist in Proto-Indo-European, it was lost early and left no trace: "In the transition from pIE through pIt. to Latin, there were lost the middle voice... the dual number; the augment... and with it the original forms of the imperfect and the pluperfect; the future and the passive, if these forms really existed in pIE." [3]

If a language does not have at hand explicit means to express a certain function, and if it becomes necessary or desirable to do so, two alternatives are possible: 1) it may use an existing form to express the new function: catachresis; or 2) it may use a longer or more descriptive phrase, perhaps employing function words or auxiliaries instead of inflection: periphrasis. Latin used both these methods to express futurity.

1) CATACHRESIS

Latin continued to use the forms which probably were employed in Proto-Indo-European to express the future.

The use of the present indicative to express futurity (the so-called *praesens pro futuro*) was widespread in spoken Latin, as can be seen in writers as far separated in space and time as Plautus, Petronius and the author of the *Peregrinatio ad loca sancta*. [4]

The *praesens pro futuro*, having never lost its popularity in the spoken language, continues today in virtually all the Romance dialects as a valid way of expressing futurity.

The Old Latin -*s*- formations with desiderative and future force did not survive beyond early Latin: "Les formes en -*s*- sont archaïques; au moment même de l'apparition des textes littéraires, elles n'ont qu'une existence précaire. Elles sont limitées à quelques verbes..." [5] Buck says that such early Latin forms as *faxō* and *capsō* "though commonly called future perfects, are simple futures formed with -*so*-, like the future in Greek and Oscan-Umbrian." [6]

---

[3] Kent 1946, 92.

[4] In the absence of any direct records of spoken Latin, these works, among others, are generally accepted as giving, at least indirectly, some indication of what spoken Latin was like. See, for example, Bal 1966, 173-178.

[5] Ernout 1945, 258. The -*s*- formations did survive in other Indo-European languages; See Buck 1933, 278-279.

[6] Buck 1933, 281.

INTRODUCTION 13

The other case in which catachresis is employed gives rise to what is thought of as the "normal" synthetic future in the third and fourth conjugations. In this instance a subjunctive is used for the future: "... à une époque antérieure à la tradition historique, le latin possédait deux subjonctifs, l'un en *ā*- (type *legās*) ... l'autre à voyelle thématique longue (type *legēs*), qu'il a répartis en conservant à l'un sa valeur de subjonctif (*legās*), et en faisant servir l'autre à l'expression du futur (*legēs*)."[7] The first person singular form of this subjunctive used as future coincided with the indicative form, and was replaced by the first person singular of the subjunctive in *ā*- (*legām*), since "... la parenté de sens du subjonctif et du futur favorisait cette substitution."[8]

2) PERIPHRASIS

While there was an alternative subjunctive which could be used as future in the third and fourth conjugations, the same was not true for the first and second conjugations. The reason is that the subjunctive in -*ā* would have been confused with the indicative for verbs of the first conjugation, while the subjunctive in -*ē* would have been confused with the indicative for verbs of the second conjugation. There could thus be only one subjunctive for each of these conjugations: subjunctives in -*ē* for verbs in -*ā*, and subjunctives in -*ā* for verbs in -*ē*. Since there was no convenient form for the future in these conjugations, a periphrasis developed in which an indicative form of the verb 'to be' **bhewə-*, **bhū-*, was added to the stem plus thematic vowel, giving such forms as **am-ā-bhwō* > *amābō*; **mon-ē-bhwō* > *monēbō*. While this form of the future originated as a periphrasis, our first examples are already synthetic, indicating that it was viewed as simply another inflected form parallel to, say, the perfect, by speakers of Latin. The case is identical in the modern Romance dialects where, for example, the speaker of Italian has no idea that the future *canterò* had its origin in the periphrasis *cantare habeo*.

These synthetic forms of the type *cantabo/audiam* have disappeared completely from all of the Romania. Among the various ways

---

[7] Ernout 1945, 253-254.
[8] Ernout 1945, 254.

available to express futurity in spoken Latin, these forms proved to be the least tenable. A number of reasons have been advanced to explain the loss of these forms: 1) The future could be adequately expressed without using a special marked form (i.e., the *praesens pro futuro*); indeed, if it were important to stress the idea of futurity, this could be done by using any one of a number of available periphrases which, at the same time, could express other subtle differences of meaning; 2) The use of two different sets of morphemes marking futurity (*amabo, -is, delebo, -is* and *dicam, -es, audiam, -ies*) was confusing. Even in works considered to be Classical Latin one finds *audibo, -is*, as well as *audiam, -ies* and *respondeam* for *respondebo*.[9] 3) Because of certain phonetic changes, e.g., [b] > [v], [ĭ] > [e], and resultant homophony, distinctions between certain tenses were lost (future/perfect: *amabit/amavit*; future/present: *dices, dicet/dicis, dicit*).

The other cases of periphrasis may be divided into two groups: 1) those composed of a participle plus a form of *sum*, and 2) those composed of a modal or auxiliary verb plus an infinitive.

1a) *Future active participle plus* sum (*called the first periphrastic conjunction in descriptions of Classical Latin*).

Not much is known about the origin of this periphrasis.[10] Up until the end of the Republican period, it was used to indicate intention, or that something was destined or about to take place.[11] This periphrasis was also used as a replacement for the future in the infinitive (*scripturum esse*), and in the subjunctive in dependent clauses (*scripturus sim, essem*).

1b) *The gerundive plus* sum (*called the second periphrastic conjugation in descriptions of Classical Latin*).

This construction had a number of uses: obligation, intention or goal with certain verbs, possibility, futurity.[12]

1c) *Future participle of* sum *plus* sum *plus infinitive*.

Translations from the Greek were responsible for the introduction of a number of periphrases into Latin. This construction was one of

---

[9] See Thielman 1885, 158.
[10] Sjögren 1906, 197.
[11] Ernout — Thomas 1953, 278.
[12] Ernout — Thomas 1953, 285-287.

the translations of Greek μέλλων 'to be destined or likely to, to be about to'.

Of the several future periphrases composed of a participle plus a form of *sum*, none has survived in Romance. Although the future active participle plus *sum* and the gerundive plus *sum* were apparently popular forms in early Latin, one can only assume that their popularity waned as other periphrases became available, until they disappeared completely from spoken Latin. *Futurus sum* plus infinitive was never a popular form, appearing only in late Latin translations from the Greek.

2a) Incipio *plus infinitive*.

Another possible translation of μέλλων was with a future form of *incipio* plus an infinitive. There is no indication that this construction was ever used in spoken Latin, and it does not occur in Romance.

2b) Volo *plus infinitive*.

Still another possible translation of μέλλων was with a construction using *volo* plus an infinitive. In this case, however, we are not dealing with a periphrasis which developed to meet the need of translating a particular construction from Greek, but rather with one that had existed for a long time in Latin. Examples of this usage occur as far back as Plautus: *Most.* 66: *ego ire in Piraeum volo* 'I want to (shall) go to Piraeus'. As Sjögren notes, this is to be interpreted as future because, as the context makes quite clear, the speaker is really quite loath to go to Piraeus.[13] This periphrasis must have been especially popular in the spoken Latin of the second and third centuries. Dacia was held by Rome from 106 A.D. to 271 A.D. and it is in Dacia — modern Rumania — that this periphrasis has survived as the predominant method of expressing futurity. That this Rumanian usage follows an unbroken line from the days of Plautus to the present must, however, remain conjectural, as we have no documentation of Rumanian until the sixteenth century.

Reflexes of *volo* plus infinitive are widely used in France. Jacques Pohl, who has made a survey of the use of this construction, finds two distributions: "... l'une, à l'est (Jura, Franche-Comté, Suisse romande), où *vouloir* s'emploie ou peut s'employer dans tous les

---

[13] Sjögren 1906, 223.

cas où le français normal emploie *aller*; l'autre, sans doute tout le domaine français, où l'emploi de *vouloir* implique que le locuteur prête aux choses, sinon une certaine volonté, du moins une certaine disposition à l'acte." [14]

In Italy reflexes of *volo* plus infinitive are used to express the future in areas as widely separated as northern Piedmont and Naples, but it is used principally in the north. [15]

In Rhaeto-Romance dialects this periphrasis also occurs along with others. [16]

Thus we see that the periphrasis with *volo* plus infinitive is a widely occurring phenomenon in Romance. It might have occurred even more widely, had *volo* been used to express 'to want' in Spanish and Portuguese rather than *quaero*. [17]

2c) Possum *plus infinitive*.

With a few verbs — notably *sperare, confidere, promittere* — *possum* was used to form a future infinitive, e.g., *posse facere* in place of *facturum esse*. Although this periphrasis was used in spoken Latin, it did not survive or further develop as an expression of futurity in any region of the Romania, but rather, in all areas, retained only its original modal meaning 'to be able to'.

2d) Debeo *plus infinitive*.

There are examples as far back as Petronius in which *debeo* is used in a potential or conjectural sense, rather than with its original meaning of obligation. For example, Petronius 67, 7: *sex pondo et selibram debet habere* 'it must weigh six and a half pounds'. While this construction is clearly not a substitute for the simple future, it does indicate an element of potentiality, which implicitly points to the future. Later examples show the futurity more clearly: Sal., *Vitae patrum*, 283: *si dixero tibi quis te occidere debebit, tu occides illum* 'if I tell you who is going to kill you, you will kill him'.

This periphrasis has survived in modern Sardinian as a normal expression of futurity (*habeo* plus infinitive is also used; see below): e.g., Logodurese *depo kantare* 'I shall sing'.

---

[14] Pohl 1961, 64.
[15] Rohlfs 1949, 387.
[16] Bourciez 1956, 623.
[17] *Voler* is used in Catalan to express 'to want' but it is not used for future periphrasis.

2e) Habeo *plus infinitive*.

Some early examples of *habeo* plus infinitive, where the context would suggest potentiality or futurity, are to be found in Cicero, *Pro Sexto* 100: *habeo etiam dicere quem ... de ponte in Tiberim deiecerit* 'I can even tell [you of one] whom he threw from the bridge into the Tiber'; *Epist. ad fam.* I, 5a, 3: *De alexandrina re causaque regia tantum habeo polliceri* 'As regards the affair of Alexandria and the king's cause, I can (shall) only promise you this'. Cicero's letters are well-known for exhibiting certain aspects of the spoken Latin of his time. Given the lack of *habeo* plus infinitive in other classical works, one has to conclude that the construction was popular rather than literary.

In the Christian writers one finds many more examples of the use of *habeo* plus infinitive. Some of the contexts require a modal interpretation, i.e., obligation, while others are clearly substituting for the simple future, as in the following example: Tert., *De res.* 40, 852a: *reputo enim non esse dignas passiones huius temporis ad futuram gloriam quae in nos habet revelari* 'for I reckon that the sufferings of this time are not worthy in respect of the future glory which is to be (will be) revealed to us'.

If one can put some degree of trust in an isolated occurrence, we also have an example of a synthetic future, forerunner of the most common Romance type, formed with *habeo* plus infinitive, in the seventh century, two centuries before what is usually considered the first Romance document, namely, the Oaths of Strasbourg of the year 842. This example occurs in Fredegar, *Chron.* I, 62: *Et ille respondebat: 'Non dabo'. Justinianus dicebat: 'Daras'.* 'And he [a defeated Persian king] kept answering: 'I will not yield [certain cities and provinces]'. Justinian kept saying: 'You will yield [them]'.[18]

As we have seen above, based on the extent of its usage, *volo* could possibly have become the generalized Romance form (compare English *will*); however, except for Balkan Romance, *habeo* plus infinitive proved to be more popular. As Bourciez puts it: "En Italie ... et dans tous les pays où s'est continuée la culture latine, *scribere habeo* ... devint l'équivalent ordinaire du futur ..."[19]

---

[18] See Valesio 1968 for a discussion of the tradition of the *daras* interpretation.
[19] Bourciez 1956, 269.

The bibliography on this, the most widespread future periphrasis, is considerable.[20] I shall here merely outline the most important aspects of its development and distribution.

Word order was extremely important, the final results depending on whether *habeo* was placed before or after the infinitive. When placed before the infinitive, *habeo* could occur alone or with a preposition *ad* or *de*. All of these possibilities have reflexes in the modern dialects.

The most usual order of *habeo* in this periphrasis was in postposition, as is shown in the synthetic futures of the principal dialects, including Portuguese, Spanish, Catalan, Provençal, French, Italian, and the dialects of the Engadine. The synthetic future also exists as an alternate form in many of the areas which prefer analytic forms.

In modern Portuguese, Old Spanish, Old Provençal, Old French, and spoken Latin, atonic personal pronouns can be placed between the infinitive and *habeo*, e.g., Portuguese *comprá-lo hei* 'I shall buy it'.

A survey of the Romania would reveal several methods of expressing futurity which we have not yet touched upon.

Dalmatian, now extinct, shows a unique case of catachresis. Simple futurity was expressed by what had been the future perfect in Latin. This form prevailed over the simple future, which, as we have noted, disappeared from the entire Romania.[21]

The remaining types of expression of futurity, which are innovations in Romance, are periphrastic: *venio (ad) cantare* and *vado (ad) cantare*.

1) *Venio (ad) cantare*. While the situation in the Rhaeto-Romance areas is rather complicated, there existing a number of future types, *venio (ad) cantare* plus infinitive proved to be one of the principal periphrases.[22] The lack of documentation for the early stages of Rhaeto-Romance is a serious obstacle to the historical study of these dialects. We have nothing before the sixteenth century. The history of *venio (ad) cantare* must thus remain obscure. From what will be said later about the history and development of *vado (ad) cantare*,

---

[20] Among others, the reader may consult: Thielman 1885; Lerch 1919; Rohlfs 1922; Löfstedt 1956; Müller 1964; Valesio 1968, 1969. These works all contain further references.

[21] Väänänen 1967, 141.

[22] Bourciez 1956, 623.

however, I believe that by analogy the lines of its development will become quite clear, if conjectural.

2) *Vado (ad) cantare*. This construction will be treated in diachronic and synchronic detail in the following chapters. However, several observations may be made at this point:

a) The periphrasis is, relatively speaking, a recent phenomenon.

b) The use of the periphrasis is restricted to western Romance (where, fortunately, we have ample documentation for Gallego-Portuguese, Spanish, Catalan, Provençal, and French). The periphrasis is *not* used in Sardinian, Italian, or Balkan Romance.

c) In those dialects in which it is used, the periphrasis has become an increasingly important method to express futurity. This trend seems likely to continue.

Chapter I

THE HISTORICAL EMERGENCE OF PERIPHRASES FORMED BY ROMANCE REFLEXES OF *VADO (AD)* PLUS INFINITIVE

In discussing the history of *vado (ad)* plus infinitive, two Latin constructions are of particular importance: the infinitive of purpose and the supine.

The infinitives in Latin originated in verbal nouns which lost some of their nominal functions and attached themselves more closely to the verbal system.[1] The original case functions were either dative or locative, both of which could express purpose. Thus constructions such as *dare bibere* 'to give (something to someone) to drink' occur in all periods of Latin. The use of the infinitive with verbs of motion was especially common in Early Latin: Plaut., *Cas.* 855: *eximus ludos visere* 'we go out to watch the games'; Plaut., *Bac.* 631: *venerat aurum petere* 'he had come to seek the gold'; Plaut., *Pseud.* 642: *reddere hoc, non perdere erus me misit* 'my master sent me to pay this back, not to lose it'.

In Classical Latin the infinitive was avoided after a verb of motion, and the accusative form of the supine (a verbal substantive of the fourth declension, occurring only in the accusative in *-um* and the ablative in *-u*) was used to denote purpose.[2]

This use of the supine can be seen in the following examples: Caes., *B.G.* 1, 30, 1: *legati ... ad Caesarem gratulatum convenerunt* 'the deputies convened in Caesar's camp to congratulate him'; Caes.,

---

[1] See Palmer 1966, 317.
[2] Woodcock 1958, 18, suggests that "The loss of perception of the original locative-dative sense of the infinitive inflection may account for the reluctance of literary Latin to avail itself of the infinitive to express purpose..."

B.G. I, 11, 2: *legatos ad Caesarem mittunt rogatum auxilium* 'they sent deputies to Caesar to ask for aid'; Livy, *A.U.C.* 3, 25: *legati ab Roma venerunt questum iniurias* 'to this camp came envoys from Rome to complain of the wrongs done'.[3]

While the supine was the preferred form for expressing purpose with verbs of motion in Classical Latin prose, in poetry the infinitive continued to be used: Verg., *Aen.* 1, 527: *non Libycos populare penatis venimus* 'we have not come to sack the homes of Libya'.

The infinitive also continued to be used in this construction in Spoken Latin: "The supine [in Vulgar Latin] disappeared from general use, being replaced, from the first century on, by the infinitive."[4] The supine may have never been a popular form in Spoken Latin, in which case the infinitive did not replace it; rather, they existed side by side for a time, the supine falling into disuse and eventually disappearing completely.[5]

Indications of the continued popularity of the infinitive in speech occur in post-classical writers who, while attempting to write Classical Latin, were unable to do so because of interference from different speech patterns: *Per.* (5th century) 25, 12: *reuertuntur in domos suas et reponent se dormito* 'they return to their houses and go back to sleep', but 27, 1: *statim unusquisque animosi uadent in Syon orare ad columnam illam* 'they all go at once with fervor to Sion to pray at the column'; Greg., *Lib. uit. pat.* (6th century) 14, 2, 50: *abiit implere iussionem* 'he went to carry out the command'; 19, 22: *audire sapientiam Salomonis adiuit* 'she went to hear the wisdom of Solomon'.

---

[3] Classical Latin was well endowed with ways to express clauses of purpose. The second example above, *legatos ad Caesarem mittunt rogatum auxilium*, could also have been expressed as follows:

legatos ad Caesarem mittunt ut rogarent *auxilium*
                                       qui rogarent
                                       ad rogandam
                                       causa rogandi
                                       rogaturos
                                       causa rogandi auxilii

[4] Grandgent 1934, 48.

[5] An exception is to be noted in that Rumanian does show reflexes of the supine; see Titkin 1904, 606: "Den Gebrauch des Supinums mit *de* zeigen Sätze wie: *éştĭ de plíns* (= *tu es à plaindre*), *bún de mîncát* (= *bon à manger*), *maşínă de presát cărămídă* 'Ziegelpressmaschine'." The infinitive, however, is also used: "Daneben Spuren des Inf.: *dáŭ de mîncáre* (= *je donne à manger*), *cásă de vînzáre* (= *maison à vendre*)."

This use of the infinitive to express purpose with verbs of motion, then, continues from Early Latin down to the Romance dialects. Examples of this usage abound in the earliest records of any length in which popular elements of speech can be found. These are the French and Spanish epics, the best known of which are the *Chanson de Roland* and the *Poema de mio Cid*. Both these works date from the first half of the twelfth century. It should be noted that there are no restrictions on the tenses of *aler* or *ir*:

Poema de mio Cid:
pres. ind: 369 *la manol va besar*
imp: 402 *a la figueruela mio Çid iva posar*
pret: 411 *a Dios se fo acomendar*
subj: 676 *vayámoslos ferir en aquel dia de cras*
imp: 898 *Si' nulla dubda id a mio Çid buscar*
fut: 1124 *hiremos veer aquella su almofalla*
inf: 1192 *quien quiere ir comigo çercar a Valencia*
fut. subj: 1696 *quando vos los foredes ferir*

Chanson de Roland:
fut: 963 *en Rencesvals irai Roland ocire*
imp: 251 *Alez sedeir, quant nuls ne vos sumunt*
pres. ind: 500 *Vait s'apuier suz le pin a la tige*
pret: 1407 *Qu'en Sarraguce sa maisnee alat vendre*
subj: 1485 *Mielz est mult que jo l'alge ocire*
inf: 2180 *Joes voell aler querre e entercer*

Something should be said here about the many different forms, in the various dialects, of what I shall for convenience continue to group under a single heading, *vado*.

The most widespread present paradigm of the verb 'to go' in the spoken Latin of the fourth and fifth centuries was composed of a combination of forms of the two verbs *vado* and *eo*: *vado, vadis, vadit, imus, itis, vadunt*, as can be found in the *Peregrinatio* and Greg., *Lib. uit. pat.*[6] Why the remaining forms of *eo* do not occur is uncertain. It may have been felt that they were too similar to desinences without stems. This, however, could also have been said about the first and second persons plural. The reflexes of this spoken Latin paradigm occur in some dialects of Italy, e.g., in Umbrian: *vo, va', va, imo, ite, vuò*. They also occur in Galician, in a few

---

[6] Rohlfs 1960, 52-56.

scattered areas of northern Portugal, and in Rhaeto-Romance dialects of the Dolomites. Old Spanish and Old Portuguese had similar paradigms; e.g., Old Spanish: *voy, vas, va, imos, ides, van.* In other areas adjustments in the paradigm were made. Forms of new verbs were used to replace the first and second persons plural. In Italian *andare* is used (forms of *andar* occur as early as the tenth century in Spain, but they never replace the forms of *eo* in the paradigm). In northern France *aler* is prevalent. In southern France and in Catalonia *anar* is the preferred form. (There is still some debate on the etyma of *aler* and *anar* which need not concern us here.) In these dialects, then, forms of two different verbs are still used in the present paradigm. In some regions analogical leveling took place. This leveling was of two types. In Sardinian the use of *andare* was generalized and used in all persons, e.g., Campidanese: *andu, ándasa, ándata, andáus, andáis, ándanta*.[7] The other type of leveling took place, at a later date, in Spanish, Portuguese, and Gascon. In these areas the first and second persons plural were replaced by the remaining forms of *vadere*, so that the present indicative of the verb *ir* is composed solely of forms of *vadere*. (This same leveling took place in Catalan, but only when the verb was used in periphrasis.)

The question as to why different verbs were used to complete the paradigm instead of the remaining forms of *vadere*, as in Spanish, Portuguese, and Gascon, remains unanswered.

The medieval Romance epics were of a popular nature and were intended to be recited or sung before the public. This accounts for the use and repetition of certain popular phrases and constructions which might have been avoided in literary works of a more learned type. The origin of the construction *vado (ad)* plus infinitive is clear. While Menéndez Pidal makes no mention of it in his study of the *Cid*, he does make several observations which are of interest here. In the *Poema de mio Cid* verbs of motion may indicate movement toward the accomplishment of some goal (while *ir* is the most commonly used verb of motion, *venir, salir,* and *exir* are also so used): 676 *vayámoslos ferir*; 655 *en Alcoçer le van çercar*. An extension of this usage leads to a periphrasis which may have been felt to be more emphatic than the simple present tense (this usage has been called 'inchoative' by Meyer-Lübke and others): "De aquí pasa a

---

[7] Wagner 1938-39, 141.

indicar la intención, como 'querer', y *la manol va besar* 369, es idéntico a *quisol besar las manos* 265; pero como esta perífrasis con *ir* o *querer* no supone que el deseo deje de estar seguido de la realización del acto deseado, sino generalmente lo contrario (298, 367, 368, 400, 402, 415), de ahí que resulte inútil, y *se van omillar* 1516 dice exactamente igual que 'se humillan'; *vay[a]mos caualgar* 1505 es igual a 'cavalguemos'; y *vayades passar* 1462 igual a 'passades'." [8]

Similar observations may be made about the corresponding constructions in the *Chanson de Roland,* where the evidence suggests even more strongly that the periphrasis was felt to be more emphatic than the simple present: a form of *aler* is used with *ferir* no fewer than thirty-five times.

In neither the French nor the Spanish of this early period is there any suggestion of genuine futurity in this periphrastic construction. [9]

In the thirteenth century examples begin to appear in which the periphrasis is seen to be neither infinitive of purpose with verb of motion, nor what Menéndez Pidal calls *perífrasis inútil,* i.e., empty of semantic content. One of the first occurrences of an innovative use of the periphrasis is in early thirteenth-century French, in *Perceval.* [10] Perceval is standing at the window, about to throw out a chess set, when a young lady calls to him from the window of an upper floor and tells him not to do so. He says: "Si vous ne venez aval, si je ves i geté." (p. 440). Since he is already at the window, he does not have to *go* anywhere in order to throw the set out. Nor is the periphrasis "empty." Quite clearly a sense of imminence or futurity is implied. An even clearer example of the loss of motion is the following, dating from the fourteenth century, where, if both

---

[8] Menéndez Pidal 1954, 350.
[9] An indication of futurity has been suggested in the *Chanson de Roland,* 270:

> E jo irai al Sarazin en Espaigne,
> Sin *vois vedeir* alques de sun semblant.

Gougenheim 1929, 98, points out, however, that this verse seems to have been altered in the manuscript, so that the earliest date we could assign to this construction would be that of the manuscript itself — late twelfth or early thirteenth century — rather than the date of composition, which was early or middle twelfth century. Furthermore, it is not at all clear that all idea of motion has been eliminated from *vois vedeir.*

[10] See also Gougenheim 1929, 97 ff.; Damourette — Pichon 1936, 97-98, 289-90.

26 THE PERIPHRASTIC FUTURES

verbs retained their literal meanings, the result would be nonsense: "La malade faire me fault/ Puis que mon gendre va venir." [11]

Damourette and Pichon point out that *aller* plus infinitive also occurs sporadically in the French of the fourteenth to sixteenth centuries as a periphrastic perfect.[12] They give a number of examples from *Melusine*, a fourteenth-century novel, quoting from Brunet's edition of 1854, which is based on a manuscript of 1478. Their case can be considerably strengthened by employing a procedure used by Colón 1961 for Catalan and Henrichsen 1966 for Provençal (see below, pp. 28-29). By comparing these occurrences with variations in other manuscripts of the period, the periphrasis can be shown to be a variant of the preterit rather than, say, the inchoative or the historical present. Louis Stouff published an edition of *Melusine* in 1932, based on a different fifteenth-century manuscript, that of the Bibliothèque de l'Arsénal. Following are comparisons of equivalent passages in the Brunet and Stouff editions:

a) BRUNET: Adoncques le varlet dist à la dame: Madame, il est temps de vous en venir quant il vous plaira; et elle prestement *va dire*: De par Dieu; puis dist au roy... (p. 18).
STOUFF: Et dist ly varlez a la dame: Ma dame, il est temps de venir quant il vous plaira, car tout est prest. Et celle *dist*: De par Dieu. Puis a dit au roy... (p. 7). (Note also in this last example the use of the passé composé for the passé simple.)

b) BRUNET: Lors le roy luy *va jurer*... (p. 19).
STOUFF: Et le roy lui *jura* ainsi... (p. 9).

c) BRUNET: ...lors *va dire* le conte a Raimondin: Beau nepveu, nous demourerons icy jusques la lune soit levée. Et Raimondin lui *va dire*... (p. 30).
STOUFF: ...et *dist* le conte a Remondin: Beau nepveu, nous demourrons cy tant que la lune sera levee. Remondin *dist*... (p. 19).

d) BRUNET: ...qu'il perdist les deux estriers, et luy *va voler* l'espée hors de la main... (p. 108).
STOUFF: ...qu'il perdy les estriers ambedux, et lui *vola* l'espee de la main... (p. 72).

e) BRUNET: Et adoncques *va venir* sa fille... qui le desarma... (p. 153).
STOUFF: Et lors *vint sa* fille, qui le desarma... (p. 107).

---

[11] *Miracles*, 334.
[12] Damourette—Pichon 1936, 117-118.

We find variations in the use of the periphrasis not only from one manuscript to another, but also within a single manuscript. In the Brunet edition of *Melusine,* for example, we find (p. 36): "Et adoncques elle *va dire* aux aultres: Je le *vois faire* parler...", where the first occurrence is past and the second implies imminence or futurity. The Stouff edition has (p. 24): "Et lors *dist* aux autres: Je le *vueil aler* a parler." (See the introduction concerning the reflexes of *volo* plus infinitive as periphrastic future.)

Innovative uses of *vado (ad)* plus infinitive also occur in thirteenth-century Spanish. The following example is from the *Primera crónica general de España,* assembled under the aegis of Alfonso X. The selection concerns one of the explanations of the death of Dido: "...desi començo a andar por la torre, llorando e dando grandes bozes llamando a so marido [who was dead], e diziendo: 'Euas tod este sacrificio quet enuio, recibo, e a mi que *uo casar* contigo otra vez'" (38a, 35). Here a sense of imminence or futurity is implied. In a later section (and a different version of the parting of Dido and Aeneas), Dido, having heard that Aeneas plans to leave for Italy, sends him a letter in which she tells him, in a passage written predominantly in the future tense: "Tu soltaras la flota quand entrares en la mar: e bien alli soltaras la postura que comigo ouiste, quebrantandola. Tu *uas buscar* los regnos de Italia que numqua uist ni sabes o son.... Busqueste por el mundo tierra, e fallestela qual tu auies mester; e agora desamparas la e *uas buscar* otra que no sabes qual la fallaras..." (40a, 9-22). Context here would allow of interpretation either as infinitive of purpose or as imminence or futurity, with the fact that the passage is set predominantly in the future favoring the latter.

Examples also occur in thirteenth-century Spanish which present the possibility of interpretations as a past tense. In *La vida de Santa María Egipciaca* (c. 1215):

> 147 En Alexandrja fue Marja,
> aqui demanda aluergueria:
> alla *va prender* ostal
> con las malas en la cal:

Here the tense of the first verb (and the verbs in the surrounding passages) would require that *va prender* be interpreted as past tense.

Similar innovations take place in thirteenth-century Provençal. An interpretation as past tense is required in the following example from *Philomena* (c. 1200): "...e *va* lhas fort *blastomar* e *reptar* e *dix que*..." (Ms. P, 2322). A comparison of the equivalent passages in the two extant manuscripts, B and P, of this work, strengthen this interpretation as past tense:

a) P, 2295: ...e *va donar* tan gran colp al cavalh de Rotlan que.lh cap li *va devalar* en .I.colp.
B: ...e *donec* tal colp al cavalh de Rotlan, que.l cap li *tolc* en un colp.
b) P, 3027: ...et aitantost elhs se *van levar* e vengron s'en a la glieysa...
B: ...*leveron* se et intreron en la glieysa...[13]

There was variation in the use of the periphrasis in Provençal, just as there was in French and Spanish. Thus we find in a mid-fifteenth-century work, *Mystères*, the periphrasis as past:

3106-7: He el no me respondet mot;
Mas me *va dire* que...

In the same manuscript we find the periphrasis as future:

6719-20: He per so que la causa me es remesa
Ieu *vau donar* ma sentencia;

In a most interesting study of *vado (ad)* plus infinitive in Catalan, Germán Colón 1959 uses three types of external evidence in demonstrating the past interpretation of the periphrasis: a) comparison of texts in Latin or Romance languages with their medieval Catalan translations, b) indications given by grammarians, and c) comparison of textual variations in different manuscripts from the same source. As an example of a) we have in the Latin text of the *Dialogues* of Saint Gregory (sixth century), 31:

Quondam vero die una Dei famula ex eodem monasterio virginum hortum ingressa est, quae lactucam conspiciens concupivit, eamque signo crucis benedicere oblita, avide *momordit*; sed arrepta a diabolo protinus cecidit.

---

[13] For further examples, see Henrichsen 1966, 358-361.

The Catalan translation (which, it should be noted, is very faithful to the original) has the following:

> Mas .I. dia, d'aquel matex monestir de les vèrgens, una servidora de Děu entrà en l'ort e viu .Ia. letuga, e cobesejà-la; e oblidà-li benesir-la ab lo seyal de la creu, e va-sse'n là e *va.y mordre,* mas tantost casec presa per lo diable.[14]

Colón gives many more examples. The evidence is conclusive for an interpretation as past tense of *vado (ad)* plus infinitive in the Catalan of this period.

Examples of this use of the periphrasis also occur in other areas, for example, in fourteenth-century Aragonese: "Et desque todas estas cosas huuo fechas el emperador fuessende a Roma e enel camino trobo sobrel Rose alli do es Leon qui eran muchos lugares chicos e derramados e *ua* los *aplegar* todos en uno e fizo hyde una grant çiudat ala qual puso nombre Leon."[15] Also in the following: "Et Nero deque fue dentro enla çiudat fizolos plegar a todos ensemble e *uales ademandar* que como eran estado tan atreuidos de mouer guerra contra el..."[16]

Italian stands apart from the other Romance dialects in the use of *vado (ad)* plus infinitive. There is no evidence of the periphrasis as future in the documents of this early period, or, for that matter, in the modern period. Two dialects are spoken on Italian soil in which we find the periphrastic perfect, but neither of these dialects is indigenous to Italy:

1) Alghero (Sardinia). This small area was colonized by Catalans under King Pedro IV of Aragon in the middle of the fourteenth century. While strongly influenced by the surrounding Sardinian dialects, it has retained many of its Catalan characteristics, including the periphrastic perfect. The paradigm used — *vaig, vas, va, anam, anats, van* — corresponds to that used in mainland Catalan when the

---

[14] *Diàlegs,* 44. Punctuation as in the original. The date of the translation is given as 1340, but the editor states (p. 14): "Respecte el temps en què pogués ésser feta aquesta versió, és posible que sigui anterior al de la copia (1340), els trets arcaics del seu llenguatge fan pensar si es tracta d'una de les escasses obres de les nostres lletres doscentistes, o de les més atansades i afins a les del doscents."

[15] *Grant cronica,* I, 10, 81.

[16] *Grant cronica,* I, 10, 83.

verb retains its full lexical value; analogical leveling did not take place when used in periphrasis, as it did in mainland Catalan (see above, p. 24).

2) Guardia Piemonte (Calabria). This is the only area in which Rohlfs found the periphrastic perfect: "Die aus dem Katalanischen bekannte Perfektumschreibung *va cantar* 'er hat gesungen', *van mirar* 'sie haben geschaut' findet sich auch auf italienischen Boden und zwar in der franko-provenzalischen Waldenserkolonie Guardia Piemontese (Kalabrien), z.B. *vo pèrdərə* 'perdei', *va trov* 'trovasti', *avè anar* 'andò', *avè štar* 'stette', *avè dùnə* 'diede', *vaŋ trov* 'trovammo', *va ciat* 'compraste', *vaŋ vənirə* 'vennero', *vaŋ pəntirə* 'pentirono', *vaŋ salút* 'salutarono'. [17]

Berchem 1968 points out that, while the history of the immigrants of the area is unclear, it is most likely that they arrived in the fourteenth century, and that, furthermore, their dialect was not, as stated by Rohlfs, Franco-Provençal, but, rather, a mixed Provençal-Piedmontese dialect. The survival of the periphrastic perfect would reinforce this view, since this construction is not characteristic of Franco-Provençal. Berchem states further: "Au moment où les Vaudois se sont installés à Guardia Piemontese, la périphrase prétéritale par *vado* + *infinitif* devait être grammaticalisée, ou, sinon, la grammaticalisation devait être nettement amorcée, car autrement il serait assez peu probable qu'un seul parler ait développé un tel procédé grammatical, alors que tous les autres parlers voisins ne le connaissent pas avec cette fonction-là." [18]

The foregoing examples are sufficient, I believe, to show: a) the period in which innovative uses of *vado (ad)* plus infinitive first begin to appear; b) the various interpretations of the periphrasis, namely, infinitive of purpose with a verb of motion, futurity or imminence, and periphrastic perfect; and c) the distribution of the various uses.

The periphrasis was used with different meanings not only from one region to another, but also within any given region. The thirteenth and fourteenth centuries constitute a period of fluctuation and variation. The reason for this is not difficult to find. The Romance dialects were in their infancy as written media and standards had not yet been established.

---

[17] Rohlfs 1949, 385.
[18] Berchem 1968, 1162.

THE HISTORICAL EMERGENCE OF PERIPHRASES   31

It would be hazardous to attempt to delimit the origin of any of the new semantic interpretations of *vado (ad)* plus infinitive based on first documented occurrences. The principal reasons for this are:

1) A considerable time lag exists between acceptance of a new form or construction in the spoken language and its first occurrence in writing.

2) A high degree of communication and mutual influence took place among the various regions of the western Romania. A number of factors are important in this regard, among them the pilgrimages to Rome, during which Portuguese, Spaniards and Catalans, as well as Frenchmen from the north and the south, traversed France and Italy; and the pilgrimages made to Santiago de Compostela by Christians from all over Europe, especially from France. Also important was the influence of the French religious orders — the Cistercians, the Carthusians, and particularly, the Cluniacensians — in Spain, Portugal, and Italy. [19]

How was it possible for a construction in the present tense — *vado (ad)* plus infinitive — to give such opposing results, i.e., future and past?

I have described above the use of the *praesens pro futuro* in Latin. Another important use of the present indicative was the historical present. The present tense was used in recalling past events in order to make the scene more vivid: "Past events may be represented as taking place before the eyes of the hearer, the temporal reference being supplied from the context. This 'Present historic' is functionally equivalent to an aoristic perfect... and it very rarely substitutes for an imperfect. Later, however (from Petronius on), more indiscriminate use is made of the present historic. This idiom was an ancient colloquial feature much utilized by the annalists. Its vividness and simplicity also made it suitable for poetry and it is particularly common in the dramatists, *the temporal framework being fixed* by introductory and concluding perfects." (Italics added.) [20] The use of the present historic has continued to the present day in all the Romance dialects. [21]

---

[19] See Vidos 1963, 395.
[20] Palmer 1966, 306.
[21] And in other languages as well; cf. English 'He calls me up at ten o'clock and tells me he can't come in tomorrow'.

The historical use of the present tense was especially prevalent in the Romance dialects during the medieval period. At the same time the emphatic or inchoative use of *vado (ad)* plus infinitive was also widely used (cf. the twelfth-century French and Spanish epics above). [22]

The frequent occurrence of *vado (ad)* plus infinitive in contexts which were clearly past, led to grammaticalization as periphrastic perfect.

Amado Alonso, in discussing grammaticalization, in general, gives the following steps in the process: a) metaphorical use of a lexical item; b) semantic change; c) grammaticalization. [23] Applying these steps to *vado (ad)* plus infinitive, we find that the metaphorical use is in two stages, namely, the present used as present historic, and *vado (ad)* plus infinitive as inchoative. The process of semantic change terminates in grammaticalization, the result of which is that the lexical term has lost its original meaning *in the given construction,* so that the metaphorical use can not be recovered by the speaker or hearer.

These same steps in the process take place in the other case, that of *vado (ad)* plus infinitive as future. A verb of motion implies movement through space. But movement through space also implies movement through time. The metaphor here substitutes movement through time for movement through space. The semantic change is, thus, from physical movement to futurity.

Having seen the sporadic and tentative beginnings of the periphrases, we shall now investigate their outcome in the various dialects.

---

[22] Perhaps a better term than 'inchoative' should be used. Gougenheim 1929, 96, found it necessary to clarify: "Nous avons employé jusqu'ici le mot 'inchoatif' pour désigner le sens de cette expression [*aller* plus infinitive]. Il importe de préciser. Le tour exprime toujours une soudaine entrée en jeu: *Il va dire* signifie non pas 'il commença à dire', mais 'il dit tout d'un coup'. (Français moderne: 'Il se mit à dire'." While standard English offers no parallel to this construction, colloquial English may express this inchoative sense in a number of ways: a) He ups and smashes everything in sight; b) He goes and blabs the secret; c) He takes and fires him on the spot.

[23] Alonso, Amado 1954, 237-239.

CHAPTER II

THE STABILIZATION OF *VADO (AD)* PLUS INFINITIVE

We have seen that during the thirteenth and fourteenth centuries *vado (ad)* plus infinitive occurred throughout Western Romance as periphrastic future and periphrastic past. During the following centuries one usage came to predominate over the other in most of the dialects. It was during these later centuries that the dialects became codified, grammars were written, and norms of acceptable usage were laid down. Certain dialects attained prestige at the expense of others. We shall look at these historical events as they relate to the evolution of the periphrases.

Gougenheim points out that for French it was only in the fifteenth century that the periphrastic future reached its full development.[1] He also lists the following important points regarding the use of the periphrasis:

1) It was quite rare in narrative, but abounded in dialogue: "Les écrivains du XVe et du XVIe siècle mettent la périphrase avec *aller* ou *s'en aller* dans la bouche des personnages qu'ils font parler, mais ne l'emploient pas pour leur propre compte."[2]

2) The periphrasis had, unlike the synthetic future, an expressive or affective value, which Damourette and Pichon would later call the "marque de l'extraordinaire".[3]

3) *Aller* and *s'en aller* were used interchangeably, sometimes within the same passage. This can be seen in the following example from the fifteenth century:

---

[1] Gougenheim 1929, 98.
[2] Gougenheim 1929, 99.
[3] Damourette — Pichon 1936, 109.

> Oyez: on vous faict assavoir
> Que on *s'en va juger* une femme,
> ....
> On la *va* ce jour *corriger* (*Moralité*, 174).

Purists began to proscribe *s'en aller* plus infinitive as *futur prochain* in the eighteenth century. Their efforts have been largely successful: "Le semi-auxiliaire *s'en aller* construit avec un infinitif ne se trouve plus guère aujourd'hui qu'a la Ire personne du singulier de l'indicatif présent.... Au XVIIe siècle, il s'employait à tous les temps et à toutes les personnes..."[4]

An important factor in the later development of the periphrasis in French was its use by writers generally considered to reflect *bon usage*. Wartburg states: "La prose artistique n'existait presque pas avant Rabelais. Les chroniqueurs du 13e et du 14e s., les nouvellistes du 15e s. écrivaient à peu près comme ils auraient parlé, sans se mettre en frais au point de vue du style. Avec Rabelais cela change."[5] Writers such as Rabelais (early sixteenth century) lent their prestige to a construction which was already accepted in the spoken language. It would now also be used in works where style and *bon usage* were important. In *Pantagruel* we find the following: "Je luy voys mander un cartel." (p. 150).

Perhaps even more important with regard to Rabelais is the fact that he does *not* use the periphrasis as past: "Le présent de l'indicatif du verbe *aller* s'emploie chez les conteurs pour marquer le début d'une action, dans le passé.... Il est à remarquer que Rabelais n'en fait jamais usage et que par là, il tranche nettement sur les autres conteurs."[6] The use of the periphrasis as past did not die out completely, however, until the early seventeenth century. Some scholars have seen a Gascon influence on French in the use of the periphrasis as past in the sixteenth century. (King Henry IV, who reigned in the latter part of the sixteenth century, was Gascon.)[7] Clearly, however, the occurrences of the periphrasis as past in this period are but remnants of an earlier usage. (For the outcome of this periphrasis in Gascon, see below, p. 40.)

---

[4] Grevisse 1964, 584.
[5] Wartburg 1965, 159.
[6] Gougenheim 1951, 136.
[7] Lanusse 1893, 429-431; Ronjat 1913, 113.

Another important factor in the further development of the periphrasis in French was the attitude of the grammarians. Gougenheim has traced their position with regard to the periphrasis.[8] Briefly, it is as follows:

Maupas was the first grammarian to comment on the construction.[9] This happened in the early seventeenth century and it is for Gougenheim "comme l'acte de naissance officiel de cette forme." Other seventeenth-century grammarians commented on the periphrasis, generally with regard to Latin equivalents: "Vulgo dicimus statim faciam hoc. *Ie m'en vay faire cecy*, quamvis non moveatur de suo loco: et sic, eo lectum, scriptum, eo vt studeam. *Ie m'en vay lire, écrire, étudier.* Propino tibi: *je m'en vay boire à vostre santé.* Dicitur etiam, *il va venir tout asteure*, statim veniet, pour dire il viendra tout asteure."[10]

In the Port Royal grammar of 1660 we also find a description of the periphrasis and a justification of its use based on Greek: "Le futur peut aussi recevoir les mesmes differences. [The difference in usage between the preterit and the present perfect *j'ecriuis / j'ay escrit* has just been discussed.] Car on peut auoir enuie de marquer vne chose qui doit arriuer bientost. Ainsi nous voyons que les Grecs ont leur *paulopost futur* μετ ὀλίγον μέλλων qui marque que la chose se va faire, ou qu'on la doit presque tenir comme faite, comme πεποιήσομαι *je m'en vas faire, voilà qui est fait.* Et l'on peut aussi marquer vne chose, comme deuant arriuer simplement, comme ποιήσω *je feray*, amabo, *j'aymeray*."[11]

This imminence of the action referred to by the periphrasis is pointed out clearly in the following: "... *aller* employé soit au Present, soit au Préterit imparfait de l'indicatif, avec les Verbes *partir, sortir*, et avec quelques autres, sert à marquer une chose qui est sur le point d'estre faite."[12]

An official name, the *futur prochain*, was given to the periphrastic future in 1753: "Un futur prochain, que les Grecs appellent *Paulo-*

---

[8] Gougenheim 1929, 99-102.
[9] Maupas 1625, 187-188.
[10] Raillet 1654, 214.
[11] Lancelot — Arnauld 1660, 104.
[12] Regnier-Desmarais 1705, 417.

post-futur, s'exprime in François par le moyen du verbe *je vais*, joint à l'infinitif." [13]

French exerted a strong influence on Italian, especially from the ninth through the twelfth centuries and, again, from the eighteenth century to the present. [14] The first period was too early for periphrastic *vado (ad)* plus infinitive to have been introduced into Italy. There is some evidence, however, that attempts were made to introduce it in the eighteenth century. [15] In a comedy, *Il Raguet*, written in the middle of the eighteenth century, the author ridicules the two young men competing for the affections of the heroine. Their speech is full of Gallicisms, most of which are misunderstood. While most of these Gallicisms are lexical, we also find the following (p. 179):

DESPINA. Ha incominciato: — Vado a dire; — e quelli:
— No, no, signor, non se ne vada, anzi la
vogliam qui. — Dicea poi: — Vengo d'intendere; —
ed essi: — In grazia, per fuggir errore,
è egli forse un paese questo intendere
del qual viene? ...

Also, later (p. 220):

ALFONSO. ...ma non dubiti, fra poco
va a venire.
DESPINA. Signora Ersilia, in grazia
uno che va a venire, va o viene?
ERSILIA. In fede mia non tel so dire.

While many lexical terms were incorporated into Italian during this period, the periphrastic constructions were not.

As we said in Chapter 1, Provençal and French used *vado (ad)* plus infinitive as periphrastic future and periphrastic past. As early as 1356, in a prescriptive grammar of Provençal, *Las flors del gay saber*, we find unnecessary periphrases proscribed for serious poetical works: "Un mot havem que soen es pedas. loqual motas vetz sostenem. per soquar es trop acostumatz. coma. *quen vas dizen.* aquel. *vas.* es pedas. o cant hom ditz. *el manet dir. aytals paraulas.* quar

---

[13] Antonini 1753, 327-328.
[14] See Tagliavini 1969, 333-334; Vidos 1963, 391.
[15] See Migliorini 1966, 511.

abasta quom diga *quem dizes. o el me dish aytals paraulas.* e jaciaysso quel sostengam. per so quar trop es acostumatz. pero pus neta es lobra qui gardar sen pot. Et aquest vici deu hom trop esquivar. en verses. et en chansos. et en autres dictatz. Pero en novas rimadas majormen can son longas. no engendara tan gran vici. coma en los autres dictatz principals. dels quals havem tractat lassus." [16]

This grammar was written for the guidance of competitors in the *Jeux floraux* in Toulouse. Provençal was already on the decline as an important literary medium, largely as a result of the Albigensian Crusade (early thirteenth century): "... the literature of the thirteenth and fourteenth centuries shows an increasing subservience to models imported from the north, and above all to the moralizing and didactic tendencies which met with clerical approval." [17]

We have seen that in French the periphrasis as future was in general use in the fifteenth century and early achieved the status of *bon usage*. The Provençal subservience to northern models, in which the periphrastic past had disappeared, and in which its use as future was accepted; the general decline of Provençal; and the fact that "the majority of those possessed by literary aspirations soon began to wield the pen in French" [18] — all contributed to the loss of the periphrastic past in Provençal. But *vado (ad)* plus infinitive has remained in general use as periphrastic future.

Studies of the early occurrences of *vado (ad)* plus infinitive in Catalan show that, in contrast with its employment in Provençal and French, it was used as periphrastic past only. It did not fulfill the competing functions of future and past. The periphrasis was grammaticalized early in Catalan, probably in the thirteenth century (see above, Chapter 1), at a time when Provençal was already under the influence of French. (It was also in the late thirteenth century that the Catalan poets began composing in their own tongue, rather than in Provençal.) Catalan remained an important medium of literature and culture until the late fifteenth century, more than two centuries longer than Provençal. While the literary use of Provençal had largely been confined to poetry, Catalan also had an important prose literature as well. It was the chancery language of the kingdom of Aragon

---

[16] Gatien-Arnoult 1843, 392.
[17] Elcock 1960, 394.
[18] Elcock 1960, 394.

and its prestige spread under King James I, who also was largely responsible for the codification of Catalan.[19] King James I also wrote his chronicles in Catalan and, at least indirectly, influenced others to write serious works in Catalan. The prestige of Catalan began to decline with the union of Aragon and Castile in 1479, the latter assuming the role of dominant partner.

I mentioned above that the Catalan poets began composing in Catalan in the thirteenth century. This is not to say that Provençal was no longer held in esteem. In *Torcimany*, a late fourteenth-century work, we find the following: "E la primera manera [of two ways of speaking in which "vices" are commonly employed] es con algú diu o posa en sos dictatz per manera de reonament ab altre aquestas seguens paraulas: 'Que.m vas dizen?' con bastaria e seria pus belh e sens pedaç que digés: 'Que.m dius?' E si be guardatz aytal sentencia, han aquestas paraulas *que.m dius?*, com aquelhas *que.m vas dizen?*, e ab aytant aquelha dicció *vas* es del tot pedaç."[20] And more specifically concerning the periphrastic past: "La segona manera es con algú posa en sos dictatz, per manera recitatoria las paraulas seguens: 'Aquelh me va dir aytals paraulas'. Con bastaria e seria pus belh e sens pedaç que dixés: 'Aquelh me dix aytals paraulas', car si be guardatz, aytal sentencia han aquestas paraulas derreras com las primeras, e ab aytant aquelhs duas diccions, co son, *me va,* romanen del tot pedaç, per tal com son superfluas."[21] While it would be better to avoid these "fillers" completely, there were times when their use was permissible: "... es escusat aquest vici si ab necessitat se han a posar paraulas, las quals en elhas matexas retengan pedaç... es escusat aquest vici en novas rimadas, e açó per lur prolixitat, per tal com en largueza de paraulas no.s poden guardar semblans cosas."[22] When these passages are compared with those cited from *Las flors del gay saber*, we can see the influence that Provençal still had on Catalan. *Torcimany* was written for the same purpose as the *Flors del gay saber* and took this work as its model. Indeed, many of its passages are simply translations from the Provençal. The proscribed constructions had completely different fortunes in the two dialects.

---

[19] See Elcock 1960, 441.
[20] Casas Homs 1956, 168.
[21] Casas Homs 1956, 168.
[22] Casas Homs 1956, 168.

The periphrastic past had already been accepted as *bon usage* in Catalan and was used by King James I himself, as well as by Ramon Llull and other prestigious writers. It is one thing to proscribe a construction which has no firmly established tradition, and quite another when not only is tradition present, but also the authority of the best writers. At any rate, purism dies hard, and we find in a fifteenth-century work, *Regles de esquivar vocables o mots grossers o pagesívols*, written in the form of the *Appendix Probi* and addressed not only to poetic usage, but to Catalan in general: "49 vaig anar e vaig venir per aní e venguí, e semblants." [23]

The periphrastic future *is* used in modern Catalan, but this is a later calque on the Castilian construction, taken into Catalan long after the acceptance in standard usage of the periphrastic past: "Hi ha un ús castellà del verb *ir* com una mena d'auxiliar, que es propaga a Catalunya amb el verb *anar* d'una manera lamentable. Imitant els castellans que diuen *Me parece que va a llover, va a llegar*, hi ha catalans que diuen *Em sembla que va a ploure* en lloc de *Em sembla que plourà* i *Va a arribar* en lloc de *Està a punt d'arribar* o *Ara arribarà*." [24]

Other grammarians, while recognizing that the use of the periphrastic future is widespread, criticize it on puristic grounds: "... con el valor de futuro inmediato, la perífrasis *anar*+infinitivo es castellanizante... aunque formas como ésta se encuentran hoy muy generalizadas, es difícil defender su legitimidad en catalán..." [25]

And on more practical grounds: "La construcció *vaig a*, amb valor de futur, a més d'esser un castellanisme molt cru, té l'inconvenient de confondre's sovint en el singular, amb el perfet perifràstic: 'Vaig a agafar una pulmonia' (castellà *voy a coger una pulmonía*) es pronuncia igual que 'Vaig agafar una pulmonia' (*cogí una pulmonía*)." [26]

Berchem ignores the Castilian origin of the periphrastic future in Catalan and the relative chronology when he says: "En catalan moderne, le futur proche exige la préposition *a* comme en espagnol: *jo vaig a cantar*. Il n'en était ainsi au moyen-âge. L'apparition de *a* pour-

---

[23] Badía Margarit 1950, 143.
[24] Jordana 1968, 27.
[25] Badía Margarit 1962, 394.
[26] Moll 1968, 168.

rait peut-être fournir un indice de plus pour fixer la date de la grammaticalization de *vado+infinitif* comme passé. Cet a évitait l'homonymie et devenait nécessaire au moment où la construction originelle tendait de plus en plus vers l'expression du passé. Le provençal n'a pas connu ce procédé thérapeutique. Il a perdu le parfait périphrastique, *vado+infinitif* continuant jusqu'à nos jours à exprimer le futur proche." [27] As will be shown below, the use of the preposition *a* in Castilian was, though obligatory in the sixteenth century, optional in the fifteenth century, a period when the periphrasis was already grammaticalized as past in Catalan. Also, as we have seen above, the French influence on Provençal may have been more important than the lack of this *procédé thérapeutique* in the loss of the periphrastic past in Provençal. At any rate, it would seem that modern Catalan is able to function with both the future and past periphrases, and that the efforts of purists to proscribe the periphrastic future will fail, as also failed earlier efforts to proscribe the periphrastic past.

In Gascon the periphrasis is also used with future and past meanings, but without benefit of a *procédé thérapeutique*: "... il est évident que la confusion entre les deux tours français 'je vais prendre le train' (je me dirige vers la gare pour prendre le train) et 'je vais prendre le train' (je ferai cette action dans un avenir proche) se complique en gascon d'une troisième interprétation possible (je pris le train). L'équivoque se résout dans la majorité des cas par le contexte.... D'ailleurs l'équivoque apparemment monstrueuse créée par la coexistence des valeurs de futur et de passé n'est pas un fait plus grave que l'autre. Mieux: la différence radicale qui sépare les deux valeurs temporelles la dissipe en général de façon évidente et immédiate." [28]

In spoken Spanish *vado* (*ad*) plus infinitive as periphrastic future was in general use in the late fifteenth century. An indication of its importance in the spoken tongue can be inferred from its position in the verbal system of Judeo-Spanish, generally regarded as reflecting

---

[27] Berchem 1968, 1166.
[28] Marquèze-Pouey 1955, 120. Some writers feel called upon to justify the treatment of Gascon as separate from Provençal; for example, see Rohlfs 1970, 4: "...il faut se rendre compte que nous n'avons pas à faire à un dialecte quelconque du domaine provençal, mais à un idiome qui dans ses nombreuses particularités, s'approche d'une vraie langue indépendante." See also Bec 1967, 47-52.

the usage of late fifteenth- and early sixteenth-century Spanish.[29] In the Judeo-Spanish of Salonika, for example, we find that occurrences of the synthetic future and the conditional are quite rare: "Dagegen ist die Umschreibung des Futurs und Konditionells durch *bo* bezw. *ia*+inf sehr häufig und scheint auf dem Wege zu sein, diese Tempora allmählich vollständig zu verdrängen."[30]

While the periphrastic future was probably common in spoken Spanish during the fifteenth century, it does not find its way into literary works until very late in the century, and then only rarely. We find, for example, in the *Celestina* (which was published in 1499) I, 195-196:

> SEMPRONIO.—... ¿quién te vido hablar entre dientes por las calles é venir aguijando como quien *va á ganar* beneficio?

And, in a later passage, 2, 191:

> MELIBEA.—Mas, si a tí plazerá, padre mío, mandar traer algún instrumento de cuerdas...
> PLEBERIO.—Esso, hija mía, luego es hecho. Yo lo *voy a mandar* aparejar.

Use of the periphrastic future becomes more common in the sixteenth century, and by the late sixteenth and early seventeenth centuries we find examples in writers of the stature of Cervantes and Lope de Vega:

Cervantes 4, 78:

> Y encomendadme a Dios en vuestras oraciones, que yo *voy a hacer* lo mismo por mi.

Cervantes I, 2, 214:

> Y según se puede colegir por su hábito, ella es monja o *va a serlo*.

---

[29] Cf. Zamora Vicente 1967, 349-377.
[30] Simon 1920, 685. This article was written at a time when Salonika was the center of a thriving Sephardic community. Before World War II there were some fifty-six thousand Jews living in Salonika (more than half the population of the city), of whom three-fourths were of Sephardic origin. There are now about 1300 Jews in the city, and Judeo-Spanish in Salonika appears doomed. Cf. Schiby 1970, 91-94.

Lope, 96:

> Hijo, el Rey me lo escribe, el Rey lo manda:
> yo *voy a responder y obedecelle*.

Lope, 249:

> No nos veremos los dos,
> que yo *me voy a morir*.

During this period we also find examples of the periphrastic future in poetry: for example, Góngora 329:

> Los dineros *van a ser*
> restituídos por vos.

The preposition *a* was not used in the construction *vado* (*ad*) plus infinitive in Old Spanish (see the examples taken from the *Cid* in the previous chapter). During the fifteenth century there was great fluctuation in usage.[31] By the sixteenth century the use of the construction with the preposition had become predominant, and after this period constructions without the preposition are not to be found in standard Spanish. In Portuguese the preposition was — and is — used only in special cases, as, for example, when another word comes between *vado* and the infinitive. An interesting case arises in the Spanish of Gil Vicente, a Portuguese dramatist who wrote in both Portuguese and Spanish. (Most Portuguese writers of the period were bilingual.) Vicente's plays were produced between the years 1502 and 1536, i.e., at a time when the use of the preposition *a* was predominant in the Spanish construction. In his works written in Spanish, Vicente uses *a* in just about half the cases. While there are numerous other indications of Portuguese influence on his Spanish, the situation with regard to the use of the preposition is less clear, and somewhat analogous to the supposed Gascon influence on the periphrastic past in French mentioned above, p. 34, i.e., we may be dealing with an older usage, rather than an outside influence: "Gil Vicente emploie aussi souvent la construction *ir buscar* que la construction *ir a buscar*, contrairement à l'usage de l'espagnol de son temps. Le lusisme est ici

---

[31] Many examples from this period are given in Cuervo 1886-1893, I, 25.

très clair, mais comme on a vu, il coïncide avec un archaïsme espagnol qui n'était pas entièrement sorti de l'usage, bien qu'il fût senti comme beaucoup plus 'marqué' que les précédents. Gil Vicente ne commet toujours pas d'"incorrection' à proprement parler; il écrit le castillan du siècle antérieur." [32]

In Portuguese we find numerous examples of the periphrastic future in the sixteenth century, for example, in the works of Vicente:

> I, 276: Me faz ir ver minha vida
> Porque *va buscar* a morte.
> I, 316: *Vou morrer,*
> Ellas hão de padecer

Vicente also uses *vado (ad)* plus infinitive as periphrastic future in Spanish:

> III, 76: Todos *van* hoy *adorar*
> al criador poderoso,
> que es nacido

In *Os Lusiadas*, an epic poem written in 1572, we find many occurrences of *vado (ad)* plus infinitive, most of which are either infinitive of purpose or historical present. Some of them, however, when they occur in dialogue, are clearly periphrastic future:

> I, 40: Mercurio pois excede em ligeireza
> Ao vento leve e à seta bem talhada
> Lhe *vá mostrar* a terra onde se informe
> Da Índia, e onde a gente se reforme.
> II, 48: Vereis a terra que a água lhe tolhia
> Que inda há de ser um pôrto mui decente,
> Em que *vão descansar* da longa via
> As naus que navegarem do Ocidente.

It would not be unreasonable to assume that the use of the periphrasis in the poetry of this period indicates a development parallel to that in Spanish, namely, that the periphrasis as future was probably common in the spoken Portuguese of the fifteenth century and found its way in literary works in the sixteenth century.

---

[32] Teyssier 1959, 334.

THE PERIPHRASTIC FUTURES

Also parallel is the lack of any mention by both Portuguese and Spanish grammarians of the periphrastic future. Whereas in French we find the construction discussed in the early seventeenth century, given an official name in the eighteenth century, and included in discussions of the verb tenses thereafter, I have been unable to find any reference to the construction during this entire period in either Spanish or Portuguese.

We have seen that *vado* (*ad*) plus infinitive is found in literary works throughout the Western Romania by the sixteenth century, in most areas as future, in some as past, and, in a few, as both future and past. The constructions were probably common in the spoken dialects a century or so earlier.

CHAPTER III

EXTENSION OF USAGE AND GRAMMATICAL TREATMENT
OF PERIPHRASTIC *VADO* (*AD*) PLUS INFINITIVE

In pursuing further our investigation of the periphrastic future in Portuguese, we may conveniently speak of three major dialect areas: Brazilian Portuguese, Peninsular Portuguese, and Galician.

A formal difference is to be noted between Galician on the one hand, and Brazilian and Peninsular Portuguese on the other, in the use of the preposition *a*. While in Brazilian and Peninsular Portuguese the preposition is used only exceptionally (see above, p. 42), in Galician, constructions with and without the preposition occur in free variation. This variation is no doubt due, in large part, to Castilian influence. Castilian is the standard language of Galicia, as this province forms part of political Spain. In any region where the inhabitants are bilingual, a certain degree of mutual interference is to be expected.[1]

Scholars writing on Brazilian Portuguese have noted the expansion of *vado* (*ad*) plus infinitive at the expense of the synthetic future: "... the absolute future (cantarei 'I shall sing') has disappeared for all practical purposes, at the colloquial speech level of our informants; the relative future [i.e., *vado* (*ad*) plus infinitive] therefore, is no

---

[1] Galician has never been successfully codified, since it has lacked the unifying influence of one great center of cultural and linguistic prestige. Gallego-Portuguese, from which Portuguese and Galician descended, was spoken until the eleventh century, when military events moved the political, cultural, and linguistic center of Portugal to the south, and Galicia "entered into a provincial decadence." (Entwistle 1962, 292). Castile later dominated the area politically and linguistically.

longer in opposition to the absolute future. In other words, the contrast between the two patterns is neutralized." [2]

Thomas notes some important exceptions: "The traditional future and conditional forms are rarely heard in speech, except the forms of those verbs whose future stem is monosyllabic. This includes, in addition to monosyllabic infinitives, three verbs which use a shortened infinitive — *trarei, farei,* and *direi* — and the verb *estar*, which often loses the first syllable in coloquial speech. To express futurity, one may use the simple present or either of two periphrastic futures: *vou falar, hei de falar.*" [3]

The use of the periphrasis has been noted in Galician and Peninsular Portuguese, but in neither area has it replaced the synthetic future to the extent that it has in Brazilian Portuguese. [4]

In a comparative study of the expression of futurity in the three areas, Jahncke confirms these observations. [5]

In all three areas, the form most often used to express futurity in the spoken language is the *praesens pro futuro*. Second, also in all three areas, is *vado (ad)* plus infinitive. The synthetic future ranks third in Peninsular Portuguese, a very poor third in Galician, and

---

[2] Kahane — Hutter 1953, 21. The principal informant for this study was a well-educated speaker from Bahia.

[3] Thomas 1966, 276. For a different view, see Mattoso Camara 1972, 148-149: "...the tense that replaces the future in colloquial speech is... the simple present itself. Frequent use of expressions with the present of *ir* is motivated by their modal and aspectual meaning. Thus what they actually replace is the simple present, not the future." I have found no other scholars who share this view. The constructions with *ir* replace the present only when the present itself is used as future. I find the positing of this intermediate step unnecessary.

[4] See García de Diego 1959, 111; Silva Dias 1959, 247.

[5] Jahncke 1966. She compares the four principal means of expressing futurity in Portuguese — the synthetic future, *praesens pro futuro*, *vado (ad)* plus infinitive, and *haver de* — by counting the number of occurrences of each in a number of different types of texts — narratives, drama, and newspapers — from each of the three areas, namely, Portugal, Galicia and Brazil. In each section the relative frequency of occurrence is stated. For the spoken language, she recorded conversations between one pair of speakers from each of the areas: those from Brazil and Portugal were of the upper class, while those from Galicia were of the working class. Because of the limited size of the corpora, especially for the spoken language, and the lack of controls on the conversations and types of texts being compared, no reliance can be placed on any statistical statements based on this study. I shall thus make only general statements regarding Jahncke's findings.

does not occur at all in the recorded conversations in Brazilian Portuguese. *Haver de* plus infinitive does not occur in any of the conversations. In all three areas, the written language is, as one would expect, more conservative, with forms of the synthetic future occurring more frequently than in the spoken tongue. Even here, however, we find that Brazilian Portuguese, particularly in the more recent works, shows a marked preference for the *praesens pro futuro* and *vado (ad)* plus infinitive, while Peninsular Portuguese and Galician use the synthetic future and *haver de* plus infinitive more freely. Thus, Peninsular Portuguese and Galician appear to be more conservative regarding the preservation of the synthetic future. It may also be that Brazilian writers are making a greater effort to reflect more faithfully in their works the patterns of the spoken tongue.

There has been, to my knowledge, no comparative study of the expression of futurity in the Hispanic dialects, such as Jahncke's for Portuguese; however *vado (ad)* plus infinitive has been widely noted, and some conclusions can be drawn on the extent of its use.

In parts of the Leonese-Asturian area, the synthetic future is rarely used: "... en Cabranes, Colunga, Infiesto, Cabrales, se sustituye por una perífrasis con *dir* [from *ir* with prothetic *d-*] que pierde su sentido de movimiento: *vo facer* 'haré'; *vamos šintar*' 'comeremos en seguida' ..."[6]

In Andalusian, as in Leonese-Asturian, the synthetic future is also rare: "El presente de indicativo llega a sustituir al futuro en varios lugares de Huelva, Sevilla y Málaga, e incluso al pretérito perfecto. La extensión de valores del presente obliga al uso de perífrasis para intensificar al propio presente; *voy a* + infinitivo es muy usada."[7]

In Aragonese, while *vado (ad)* plus infinitive occurs as periphrastic future, its role is less important than in the other Hispanic dialects. The reasons for this are to be found in two of the major characteristics of Aragonese: archaism and strong Catalan influence.[8] In some areas, for example, Alta Ribagorza, the principal use of *vado*

---

[6] Zamora Vicente 1967, 209. Note the lack of the preposition *a* in this construction. This is the general usage throughout Asturias.

[7] Zamora Vicente 1967, 330.

[8] In comparison with Aragonese and other Hispanic dialects, Castilian, which, as Standard Spanish, has exerted some degree of influence on all the other dialects of the peninsula, has often been characterized as innovative. See, for example, Entwistle 1962, 107; Baldinger 1963, 40.

(*ad*) plus infinitive is, as in Catalan, to form the periphrastic perfect: "Al pretérito perfecto castellano corresponde en nuestra región el *pretérito perifrástico* formado con 'aná' (= ir), lo mismo que en el catalán y gascón. A diferencia del catalán, en que, además del pretérito perifrástico, existe uno sintético (por ejemplo rompí), las hablas de nuestra región forman el pretérito exclusivamente mediante la perífrasis..."[9]

While continuous documentation is lacking in Leonese-Asturian, Andalusian, and Aragonese from the time of the first documented occurrences of periphrastic *vado* (*ad*) plus infinitive, we have, in Castilian, a continuous literary production. An attempt has been made to document the fluctuating patterns of usage in the expression of futurity in Castilian from the seventeenth century to the present.[10]

Following is a resumé of these findings (figures represent percentages of total expressions of futurity):

	17th cent. Cervantes	Lope	19th Bretón	Lorca	20th Modern
synthetic future	82.5	80	82	78	62
haber de plus inf.	17.5	18	12	4	1
vado (*ad*) plus inf.	—	2	6	15	33
praesens pro futuro	—	—	.3	3	4

While the synthetic future is still the most common written expression of futurity, its use has decreased considerably. The use of *haber de* plus infinitive has also decreased, almost to the point of complete disappearance. The employment of the *praesens pro futuro* has increased somewhat, and that of *vado* (*ad*) has increased greatly. There were some cases of the semi-synthetic future (in which

---

[9] Haensch 1960, 113.

[10] Sáez-Godoy 1967-68. This study suffers from the same shortcomings as those noted for Jahncke 1966. It does, however, treat only one genre — drama (which the author analyzes because it approximates the spoken language more closely than other written forms) and one dialect: standard written Castilian. Three periods are analyzed: early seventeenth century; nineteenth century; and early and mid-twentieth century. All expressions of futurity were noted and percentages calculated. While reliance can not be placed on absolute percentage figures as representative of the spoken language, the changes in percentages from one period to another indicate some definite trends (keeping in mind that written language generally lags behind the spoken language in the use of innovations).

EXTENSION OF USAGE AND GRAMMATICAL... 49

a pronoun is placed between the infinitive and the present tense form of *haber*) in the works of Cervantes. These were counted along with the synthetic future. This construction was on its way to extinction in Cervantes' day and, indeed, has disappeared from Spanish (it is still retained in Portuguese). The figures in the last column are questionable if actually taken as representative of the spoken language. One feels that the figure for the synthetic future is far too high, and that of the *praesens pro futuro* is far too low. Sáez-Godoy recognizes this, and another study of futurity, in tales taken from the oral tradition, confirms it. [11] Here the figures are the following:

> synthetic future   27 %
> *praesens pro futuro*   36 %
> *vado (ad)* plus inf.   37 %

The discrepancy between these figures and those pertaining to the modern authors in Sáez-Godoy 1967-68 should serve as further warning against taking any written sample of language as representative of the spoken tongue (see also below, p. 50).

In commenting on general Latin-American usage, Kany says the following: "The locution *ir a* + inf. to replace the future is common everywhere, but in popular American Spanish it has extended its domain beyond its normal usage in Spain." [12] Numerous authors confirm Kany's observation. [13]

Relating the difference in usage between the written and spoken word to the use of the synthetic future, Lope Blanch says: "En la lengua hablada puede observarse una repugnancia muy marcada hacia las formas del futuro. El pueblo prefiere usar las perífrasis de valor futuro.... No sucede lo mismo en la lengua escrita, que mantiene en pleno uso este tiempo." [14]

---

[11] Cf. Hunnius 1967-68; this study is based on fifteen tales taken from Espinosa 1946.

[12] Kany 1951, 154-155. The Spanish spoken in America, for whatever reasons, seems to conform less to the written language than does Peninsular Spanish: "...the gap between the spoken tongue and the literary language is considerably wider in America [than in Spain]. When taking pen in hand the Spanish-American author withdraws more completely from linguistic reality than does the Spaniard." (Kany 1951, ix).

[13] Among them, Padrón 1950, 166; Zamora Vicente 1967, 434; Montes 1962; Lope Blanch 1953, 73.

[14] Lope Blanch 1953, 73.

A further example of this gap between written and spoken usage can be seen in yet another short study with interesting implications.[15] Grimes has compared the methods used to express futurity in two modern works. The first is a novel, *Pedro Páramo* by Juan Rulfo, a Mexican novelist "que tiene fama de *recrear* o reproducir el habla popular por su íntimo contacto con los campesinos de Jalisco..."[16] Only dialogue portions of the novel are used in the comparison. The second work analyzed is *Los hijos de Sánchez* by Oscar Lewis, which consists entirely of transcriptions of recorded conversations with the members of a lower-class family. The difference in usage is striking:

	Pedro Páramo	Sánchez
synthetic future	84.3 %	7.9 %
praesens pro futuro	—	18.3 %
vado (ad) plus inf.	14.1 %	67.3 %[17]

The position of the synthetic future is reduced even further when we consider that in well over half of the cases it is used in a formulaic expression with the verb *ver*: *ya verás*, etc.[18]

While Grimes realizes that it might be too hasty to state any positive conclusions based on such a small amount of evidence, he does cast doubt on Rulfo's reputation as a writer who faithfully represents peasant speech: "... valdría la pena profundizar este estudio analizando otros aspetos [*sic*] en las obras de Rulfo y en el habla popular reproducida en cintas. Tal vez la crítica mexicana ha 'jumped the gun' en destacar a Rulfo como experto en el habla popular, por lo menos en lo que se refiere a la sintaxis."[19]

In a discussion of *vado (ad)* plus infinitive in modern French, Imbs says the following: "Dans la langue de la conversation le futur périphrastique tend à remplacer le futur simple; il doit cette exten-

---

[15] Grimes 1967-68.
[16] Grimes 1967-68, 352.
[17] I have disregarded as statistically unimportant the few occurrences of other constructions which Grimes interprets as expressions of futurity: *venir a* plus infinitive, *volver a* plus infinitive.
[18] In his study of the expression of futurity in Colombian Spanish, Montes 1962, 538-540, also notes this use of the future in "fórmulas hechas." All of the examples he gives use a form of *ver*. Surprising in Montes' study is the omission of any mention of the role of the *praesens pro futuro*.
[19] Grimes 1967-68, 352.

sion à sa forme expressive, mais aussi aux conditions même de la conversation, dans laquelle l'avenir est normalement envisagé dans le prolongement ou comme une suite logique du présent." [20]

Other scholars have noted the expansion of *vado (ad)* plus infinitive at the expense of the synthetic future in French. [21] Regarding the frequency of usage, one finds the following remarks concerning "le français élémentaire": "Cette périphrase fait concurrence à la forme simple du futur. Les statistiques établies lors de l'élaboration du 'français élémentaire' montrent que, pour l'expression du futur *une fois sur trois* la périphrase *aller + infinitif* se substitue au futur simple et que, pour l'expression du futur dans le passé, *une fois sur deux* le conditionnel présent est remplacé par la périphrase..." [22]

Half a century ago, Bauche was saying, in perhaps somewhat exaggerated terms: "Le futur traverse une crise en LP [langage populaire].... Le futur constitué selon la formation romane... semble reculer en LP devant le futur de forme germanique, c'est-à-dire formé avec un auxiliaire..." [23] Bauche ends his book with a list of predictions; among them: "Disparition possible du futur et son remplacement par un futur composé à la façon germanique et slave, grâce à l'adjonction d'un auxiliaire (vouloir, aller, devoir)." (p. 188). Bauche's prediction has not yet come true, at least for standard French. A survey of studies on other Gallo-Romance dialects is inconclusive with regard to the extent of usage of *vado (ad)* plus infinitive. It is mentioned just in passing, if at all, and it apparently plays no important role in the verbal system of these dialects (to the same degree that it does, say in Leonese). [24]

In French-speaking areas outside Europe no consistent pattern emerges. For Quebec, little is to be said regarding the periphrasis. Studies on Canadian French imply that the situation parallels that of France, as special note is made only of divergences from the

---

[20] Imbs 1960, 57. If what the author says is correct, then, in conversation, the contrast between the *futur* and the *futur prochain* is neutralized. See above, pp. 45-46, for neutralization of the contrast in Brazilian Portuguese.

[21] See, for example, Pulgram 1963, Pulgram 1967, Chevalier *et al.* 1964, 332.

[22] Chevalier *et al.* 1964, 332.

[23] Bauche 1929, 119-120 (this book was first published in 1920).

[24] See, for example, Bjerrome 1957, 110 (Switzerland); Chaurand 1968, 205-206 (Picardy).

standard.[25] In other regions, the role of the synthetic future has largely been taken over by *vado (ad)* plus infinitive. Thus, we find in Louisiana: "LaF [Lafayette dialect, spoken in three parishes centering on the town of Lafayette, in south-central Louisiana] usage favors the synthetic future when irregular verbs are involved, the analytic or periphrastic with regular verbs; indeed, there are, in our corpus, less than ten regular futures..."[26]

In the French dialect of Old Mines, Missouri, the synthetic future has also been largely replaced by *vado (ad)* plus infinitive.[27] In these areas of Louisiana and Missouri, as opposed to Quebec, French is neither an official nor a dominant language. It is not the language of culture or of education. It is used only in the spoken form, hence its evolution has gone unchecked by the conservative influence of the written word. Thus, tendencies already discernible in Standard French have proceeded at a faster rate.[28]

In Haiti, while French is "la langue de l'administration, de la justice, de l'enseignement," the overwhelming majority of inhabitants speak only Haitian Creole (even in Port-au-Prince, only slightly over 10 % of the inhabitants speak French as the principal language in the home).[29] In his analysis of Haitian Creole, Hall lists three variants of the future tense prefix: *a-, ava-, va-* (all from *aller*) as the only type of future formation, e.g., *m-ava-ouvri pòt-la* 'I'll open the door'.[30]

The history and patterns of usage of *vado (ad)* plus infinitive seem clear and quite parallel for French, Spanish, and Portuguese. In the three dialects we find the tentative beginnings of the construction in the thirteenth and fourteenth centuries, widespread use in the spoken

---

[25] See, for example, Massignon 1962.

[26] Juilland — Conwell 1963, 156. Cf. Thomas' statements above, p. 46, on Brazilian Portuguese. Thomas notes the use of the synthetic future with verbs having monosyllabic stems. Most French irregular verbs would also fit this criterion. Juilland — Conwell also list nine additional parishes which other studies have shown to prefer the analytic future (p. 156, n).

[27] Thogmartin 1970, 49-50.

[28] In northern Africa, some regions of which — Algeria, Morocco, and Tunisia — are bilingual in Arabic and French, substratum influences may help to account for this same loss of the synthetic future. Arabic does not distinguish morphologically the present from the future. Thus, the tendency is to use the *praesens pro futuro*. *Vado (ad)* plus infinitive is also used. See Lanly 1970, 210-211, 260-261.

[29] Pompilus 1961, 19.

[30] Hall 1953, 65.

tongue in the fifteenth, acceptance into literary works in the sixteenth and seventeenth centuries, and continual expansion up to the present day. In the overseas regions (with the possible exception of Quebec) the construction has increased its role with respect to the mother countries, to the point that in some dialects the synthetic future is rarely, if ever, found in speech. [31] *Vado (ad)* plus infinitive has achieved an importance in French, Spanish, and Portuguese that deserves to be accounted for in the grammars of these languages. I share Martinet's view: "Les formes verbales composées du type *j'ai donné, je vais donner* font partie du système verbal au même titre que les formes simples, et une étude des conditions d'emploi doit les placer toutes sur le même plan." [32] Constructions of the type *j'ai donné* are, indeed, treated as part of the verbal system in the grammars of all the Romance dialects; the compound tenses play an important part in the verbal paradigms. The position of *vado (ad)* plus infinitive in the system is quite different. In consulting a number of reference works for each of the three dialects under question, one is struck by the uneven treatment given the periphrasis. [33] In all the French works consulted, the use of the construction is noted: *aller* is called an auxiliary verb (Dauzat, Wartburg — Zumthor, Académie française, Gougenheim, LeBidois — LeBidois), a semi-auxiliary (Chevalier *et al.*, Grevisse), or a secondary auxiliary (Mauger). All the French works

---

[31] Comparisons of the frequency of usage from one language to another are not possible at the present time. Using the data in the frequency dictionaries compiled by Juilland and his colleagues (Juilland — Chang Rodríguez 1964; Juilland *et al.* 1970), which are based on comparable corpora, evenly divided among five genres (plays, fiction, expository prose, periodicals, and scientific writings), one can only state that a form of the verb *ir* is used in written peninsular Standard Spanish nearly twice as often as a form of *aller* in written Standard French (2060 occurrences to 1201), while in an auxiliary function (presumably including such constructions as *vado* plus gerund), a form of *aller* in written Standard French is used more than twice as often as a form of *ir* in written peninsular Standard Spanish (565 to 260). The frequency dictionary of Portuguese has not yet appeared.
[32] Martinet 1958, 312.
[33] For French: Académie française 1932; Gougenheim 1938; Dauzat 1958; Wartburg — Zumthor 1958; Chevalier *et al.* 1964; Grevisse 1964; LeBidois — LeBidois 1967; Mauger 1968. For Spanish: Lenz 1925; Alonso — Henríquez Ureña 1959; Real Academia Española 1959; Gili y Gaya 1960; Criado de Val 1966; Alonso, Martín 1968; Seco 1968; Bello 1972. For Portuguese: Silveira Bueno 1958; Almeida Tôrres 1965; Azevedo Filho 1968; Bechara 1968; Chaves de Melo 1968; Victoria 1968; Cunha 1970; Rocha Lima 1972.

refer to this construction as *futur prochain* (or *proche*). But in only two of them is the construction actually included as part of the verbal paradigm (Chevalier *et al.*, Dauzat).

Among the Spanish works consulted, three make no mention whatever of *vado* (*ad*) plus infinitive (Real Academia, Alonso — Henríquez Ureña, Bello); two of them mention the *futuro inmediato* while avoiding the term 'auxiliary' (Alonso, Lenz); two others (Gili y Gaya, Criado de Val) use the term 'auxiliary' and refer respectively to "la intención, la realización inminente, o el principio de una acción" (Gili y Gaya 1960, 139), and to "la voluntad o disposición de ánimo para ejecutarlo [el hecho]... expressiones incoativas... acción que comienza a efectuarse, bien en la intención o creencia sujetiva, bien en la realidad exterior" (Criado de Val 1966, 96, 100); Seco, using neither the term 'auxiliary' nor *futuro inmediato* discusses *vado* (*ad*) plus infinitive only with reference to *haber de* plus infinitive: "... este mismo sentido [de intención o propósito futuro] lo expresa de modo más eficaz [que *haber de* + infinitivo] la perífrasis formada con *ir a* y un infinitivo" (Seco 1968, 173). Among Spanish grammarians, then, there seems to be no concensus on the acceptance of *vado* (*ad*) plus infinitive into the verbal system.

Of the works consulted for Portuguese, five make no mention of *vado* (*ad*) plus infinitive (Almeida Tôrres, Victoria, Azevedo Filho, Bechara, Rocha Lima); Bechara and Rocha Lima do treat *ir* as an auxiliary in the construction *ir* plus gerund; two others (Silveira Bueno, Chaves de Melo) note the use of *ir* plus infinitive when discussing auxiliaries, but make no further reference to it; only one (Cunha), who refers to *ir* as an auxiliary, discusses the use of the construction: "... para exprimir o firme propósito do executar a ação, ou a certeza de que ela será realizada em futuro proximo..." (Cunha 1970, 268). Thus, *vado* (*ad*) plus infinitive finds even less acceptance among the Portuguese than among the Spanish grammarians.

From the observations of present-day usage discussed above, it becomes evident that the different treatments accorded the periphrastic future are a matter of grammatical tradition more than a description of actual usage. Differences in employment among the three dialects regarding this construction are slight, and are of degree, rather than of kind. However, grammatical treatment is another matter. As we have seen in Chapter 2, a tradition of treating *vado* (*ad*) plus infinitive as an auxiliary in French was established in the early seventeenth century. This tradition has continued to the present day. In Spanish and Portuguese no such tradition exists, and, as a result, the majority of Spanish and Portuguese grammarians inadequately appreciate the importance of *vado* (*ad*) plus infinitive as an expression of futurity.

While there is little concensus on the treatment to be accorded *vado* (*ad*) plus infinitive in the works consulted for Spanish and Portuguese, we do find rather general agreement on what tenses make up the indicative paradigms.[34] Although terminology may differ, it is generally agreed that the paradigm is composed of five simple and five compound tenses in Spanish, and six simple and four compound tenses in Portuguese. For French, also, we find general agreement on what forms make up the paradigm. Besides five simple and five compound forms, five *formes surcomposées* are generally recognized (exceptional, are, as noted above, Chevalier *et al.*, who add the *futur périphrastique*, and Dauzat, who adds the *futur proche* and the *passé proche*).[35]

Verb paradigms and the categories for which they are inflected are stable; hence, it seems unlikely that *vado* (*ad*) plus infinitive will ever be represented as a compound tense in the Spanish and Portuguese verb paradigms, although, as we have seen, in the spoken tongue it plays a more important role than the synthetic future. In French, while the construction is used no more frequently than in Spanish or Portuguese, its use is commented on in all the works consulted, and is actually added to the verb paradigm in two of them. The importance of an established position (and, thus, an acceptable term) is pointed out in the rather defensive statement of one of the Portuguese grammarians: "Temos para nós que é útil e muito legítimo distinguir entre *locução verbal* e *tempo composto*.... A razão é que os tempos compostos fazem parte da conjugação normal, têm cada qual seu nome (v.g., 'pretérito perfeito composto'...) dentro da

---

[34] See Appendices 1 and 2.

[35] See Appendix 3. The similarity of the verb paradigms of French, Spanish, and Portuguese is somewhat masked by the different terminology, as can be seen by comparing Appendices 1, 2, and 3. Formally, there are only two basic differences: 1) the *formes surcomposées* of French have no counterpart in Spanish or Portuguese, and 2) the Latin pluperfect survives in Portuguese (*cantara*), whereas it was lost in French, and has taken over a past subjunctive role in Spanish, where it alternates with the inherited pluperfect subjunctive (*cantase*).

conjugação, ao passo que as locuções verbais constituem cada uma sua conjugação inteira e nascem das necessidades de expressão mais complexa, em que se busca traduzir o 'aspecto verbal'." [36]

The traditional number of tenses and their names are of little importance in the treatment of verbs in transformational grammar. Thus, we might expect to find the periphrastic future analyzed with less reliance on tradition, and more in accord with actual use. We shall see if this proves to be the case.

In transformational grammar, usually only two tenses are spoken of: past and present, or past and non-past. The reason for distinguishing only these two tenses is that "whereas the past tense does typically refer to 'before-now', the non-past is not restricted to what is contemporaneous with the time of utterance: it is also used for 'timeless' or 'eternal' statements... and in many statements that refer to the future..." [37] In the Romance dialects, past may be further sub-divided into imperfect and perfect aspects. The basic tenses in transformational grammar are, thus, what traditional works call the present, the imperfect and the preterit. Except for the synthetic pluperfect in Portuguese, these are the only indicative tenses which have survived from Latin in the three dialects under discussion. All other tenses are Romance creations and are accounted for in transformational grammars in the auxiliary component. [38]

---

[36] Chaves de Melo 1968, 166-167. The reasoning here is circular. It should also be pointed out that *vado* (*ad*) plus infinitive does not have a "conjugação inteira," i.e., it is not conjugated in all the tenses, but only in the present and the imperfect.

[37] Lyons 1968, 306. As we have seen above, pp. 25-32, the non-past may also refer to the past. We might call this, borrowing a phrase from Bull 1965, 160, a "non-systemic" use of the non-past.

[38] There are two theoretical positions on the representation of the auxiliary component: it may be treated 1) as a constituent of the sentence (Chomsky 1965; Jacobs — Rosenbaum 1968; Burt 1971), or 2) as a constituent of the verb phrase (Dubois — Dubois-Charlier 1970; Liles 1971; Hadlich 1971):

```
1)         S                    2)         S
         / | \                            /   \
        NP Aux VP                        NP    VP
                                              /  \
                                            Aux   V
```

The works consulted for French and Spanish have all preferred the second alternative.

The French verb phrase has been described as follows: [39]

Verb Phrase → Auxiliary + Verbal [40]
Auxiliary → Tense + (Perfect) + (Modal) + (Perfect)
Tense → ({Future / Subjunctive}) + {Present / Past} + Person + Number
Past → {Imperfect / Preterit}
Perfect → {avoir / être} + Past Participle
Modal → {Mode / Aspect} + Infinitive
Mode → *pouvoir, devoir*
Aspect → *aller, être en train de, venir de, être sur le point de*

All the morphemes included under Tense are affixes, as are the morphemes signaling the past participle and the infinitive. When a modal, or *avoir*, or *être* is employed, an ordering rule shifts the infinitive or past participle morpheme to the verb stem generated by the Verbal. The sentence *Les enfants mangeront des fruits* may be diagrammed as follows:

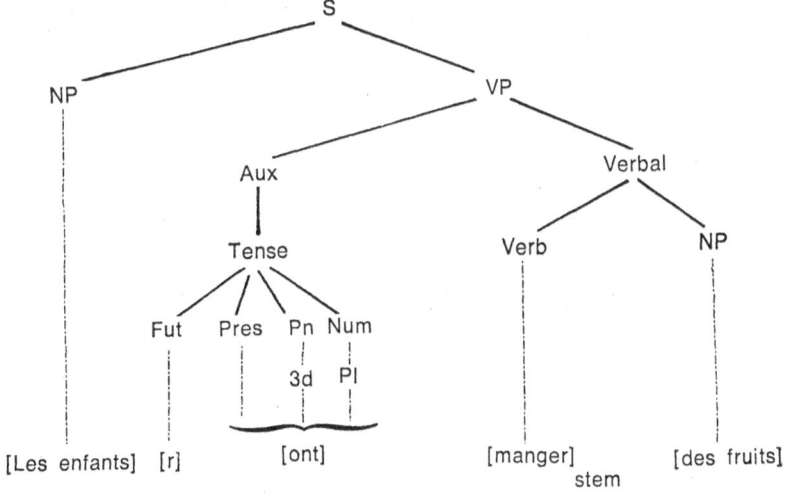

---

[39] Dubois — Dubois-Charlier 1970, 71-112. I have modified the authors' terminology to correspond to that used in English transformational grammar, preferring, for example, 'verb phrase' to *syntagme verbal*.

[40] For present purposes, it is sufficient to note that Verbal supplies the verb stem. A complete rewrite rule would be:

By way of comparison, the representation of *Les enfants vont manger des fruits* is the following:

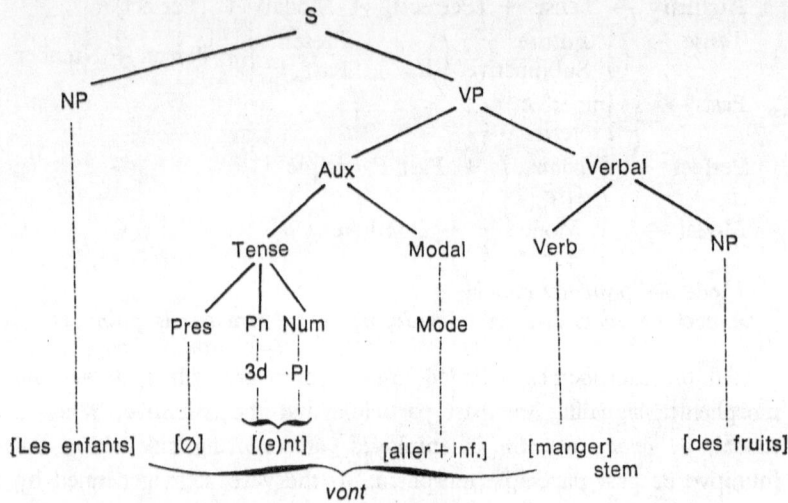

A type of analysis such as the foregoing does not go beyond the grammars cited in the preceding chapter in explaining the function of *vado (ad)* plus infinitive in the verbal system. The importance of the periphrasis in expressing futurity is ignored. *Aller* is simply placed together with other auxiliaries that govern an infinitive. Restrictions on the tenses in which *aller* can be used in its auxiliary function are not adequately accounted for, although the authors do say: "Les modaux et les aspectuels comportent des traits qui déterminent des règles contextuelles à l'intérieur du constituant Aux et qui limitent le choix de certains constituants de [Temps]. Par exemple: *aller* a le trait [+ futur] qui exclut Futur ou Subj dans la réécriture de [Temps]." [41]

$$\text{Verbal} \rightarrow \begin{Bmatrix} \text{Copula} + \begin{Bmatrix} \text{Noun Phrase} \\ \text{Adjective Phrase} \\ \text{Prepositional Phrase} \end{Bmatrix} \\ \begin{Bmatrix} \text{Transitive Verb} + \text{NP} \\ \text{Intransitive Verb} \end{Bmatrix} + \begin{pmatrix} \text{Prepositional} \\ \text{Phrase} \end{pmatrix} \end{Bmatrix}$$

Following the conventions of transformational grammar, terms within parentheses are optional: braces indicate that one, and only one, of the terms enclosed by them is to be chosen.

[41] Dubois — Dubois-Charlier 1970, 105.

In works on Spanish transformational grammar, *vado [ad]* plus infinitive has not been adequately treated. In one of the earliest transformational analyses of Spanish verb forms, Wolfe considers only *poder* and *deber* as modal auxiliaries. He does not, however, try to account for all possible verb forms and states that the exclusion of certain forms "does not imply... that they could not be incorporated into the type of grammar which is developed in my study..." [42]

In their contrastive study of Spanish and English, Stockwell *et al.* do not include modal auxiliaries in the discussion of the Spanish verb phrase, although they do include them in the English verb phrase. Their justification for this treatment of Spanish is that verbs such as *poder, querer,* and *deber* "share almost none of the modal characteristics of English; they have full paradigms for person, number, tense, and aspect; they accept objects like other transitive verbs; they allow the secondary modifications of other verbs; in short, they are simply verbs which happen to carry lexical meanings that overlap with the meanings of English modals." [43]

The authors include two sets of modifications in the auxiliary component: primary and secondary. The primary modifications, which are obligatory, are aspect (perfective and imperfective) and tense (past and non-past). The secondary modifications, which are optional, are duration (*-ndo* forms), anteriority (compound perfect forms), and subsequence (future and conditional). The authors propose the following rewrite rules:

Verb Phrase → Auxiliary + Verbal
Auxiliary → Aspect (*haber* + *-do*) (*estar* + *-ndo*)
Aspect → { Perfective / Imperfective }
Imperfective → { Past / Non-past } (*-haber*)

With reference to subsequence, the authors add in a footnote: "In Spanish, the construction with *ir a* (*Voy a salir*) is also a mark of subsequence." [44] They offer no further discussion or explanation of

---

[42] Wolfe 1966, 3.
[43] Stockwell *et al.* 1965, 165. The authors make no reference to English 'going to' plus infinitive, nor do the authors of any other transformational analyses of English which I have seen.
[44] Stockwell *et al.* 1965, 148.

this observation. One can only wonder what rules account for the subsequence of such a sentence as *Voy a salir*. Also, it should be pointed out that the construction *may* be a mark of subsequence, but only in the present and imperfect: a sentence such as *Fui a ayudarle* is not marked for subsequence. On the other hand, the authors would be unable to assign different descriptions to the two possible interpretations of such a sentence as *Voy a ayudarle todos los días* (I go and help him every day' and 'I'm going to help him every day'). Dubois — Dubois-Charlier have commented on the double usage which is at the root of this ambiguity: "Certains *modaux (aspectuels* et *modalités)* sont homonymes de verbes 'au sens plein', c'est-à-dire de verbes qui peuvent être insérés à la place de V. Les modaux sont dominés par le symbole Aux, alors que V est dominé par [Verbal]. La distinction est assurée par le fait que les modaux et les aspectuels peuvent être suivis du verbe homonyme: *Je vais aller le chercher...*".[45] Such an explanation is, of course, impossible in the framework provided in Stockwell *et al.*, since they use no modal component in the auxiliary.

In the most recent transformational grammar of Spanish, the author has, indeed, included a modal component of the auxiliary: [46]

Aux → Aspect Tense (Modal) (*haber -do*) (*estar -ndo*)[47]
Aspect → { ± perfective / + subsequent }
Tense → ± past

Hadlich, after noting that Spanish grammarians agree on the existence of auxiliary verbs, but disagree on which verbs belong in this category, gives his own list:

Modal → *poder, soler, haber de, parecer, deber (de), acabar de, tener que, tratar de, dejar de.*

---

[45] Dubois — Dubois-Charlier 1970, 105.
[46] Hadlich 1971, 59.
[47] Hadlich actually gives a more complicated rule:

Aux → Asp T (M -r) (*haber -do*) (M -r) (M -r) (*estar -ndo*)

The author explains that this rule is probably over generalized, and that the simpler rule given above may reflect the facts more accurately. A second rule could be added to allow any verb to receive a second modal. This would permit two modals to occur together as in *Suele poder terminar*.

It is surprising that in such an extensive list, *ir a* is not included. I believe that this may have been an oversight on Hadlich's part, since *acabar de*, which parallels *ir a* and has the same tense restrictions, is included. Otherwise, *ir* must be considered a main verb, i.e., one which is generated by the verbal component, rather than the auxiliary. If this is the case, then Hadlich's analysis contains the same inadequacies regarding the periphrastic future as those pointed out in Stockwell *et al.*

Let us suppose that the domain of *vado (ad)* plus infinitive continues to expand in all the areas described in earlier chapters, neutralizing any contrast that might have existed with the synthetic future (as has already happened in Brazil), until its status as an expression of futurity can no longer be ignored by grammarians; or, alternatively, let us suppose that grammarians presently wished to modify their descriptions of the verbal systems we have discussed. Revising the traditional grammars to reflect this usage would be a simple task, consisting of merely adding a new tense to the paradigm. This has already been done for French by Dauzat 1958 and Chevalier *et al.* 1964. The difficulty lies only in overcoming traditional terminology used over many centuries.

How would this new situation be accounted for in transformational grammar? Let us see what modifications might be necessary in the rules given by Dubois — Dubois-Charlier and Hadlich. [48]

In order to reflect the function of *vado (ad)* plus infinitive relative to the position of the synthetic future, the analysis would have to treat the two constructions at the same level, i.e., in the component of the auxiliary called tense by Dubois — Dubois-Charlier and aspect

---

[48] A comparison of these two grammars reveals some basic differences: subjunctive, person, and number are included in the base rules by Dubois — Dubois-Charlier, and in the transformational rules by Hadlich; the two perfect components in the former account for the *formes surcomposées* in French, while the *(estar -ndo)* component in the latter accounts for the progressive tenses in Spanish. Some basic similarities are also to be noted: both use three basic tenses; *futur* is the same as 'subsequent', and both are used in the same tenses. No transformational grammar of Portuguese, to my knowledge, has yet been published; however, differences between Spanish and Portuguese verb phrases at the phrase structure level are rather superficial (consisting principally of the addition of *tener* as an auxiliary, and the use of the synthetic pluperfect), and there would be little difficulty in modifying the Spanish rules so as to make them fit Portuguese.

THE PERIPHRASTIC FUTURES

by Hadlich (or what could be called tense-aspect in both analyses). Hadlich's rules, revised, would be:

$$\text{Aux} \rightarrow \text{Asp T (M)} \ (haber \ \text{-}do) \ (estar \ \text{-}ndo)$$
$$\text{Asp} \rightarrow \left\{ \begin{array}{l} \pm \text{ perfective} \\ + \text{ subsequent} \end{array} \right\}$$
$$\text{Sub} \rightarrow \left\{ \begin{array}{l} \text{-}haber \\ ir \ a \end{array} \right\} \text{infinitive}$$
$$\text{T} \rightarrow \pm \text{ past}$$

These rules would then generate the two sentences 1) *Los niños comerán la fruta*, and 2) *Los niños van a comer la fruta* as follows:

1)

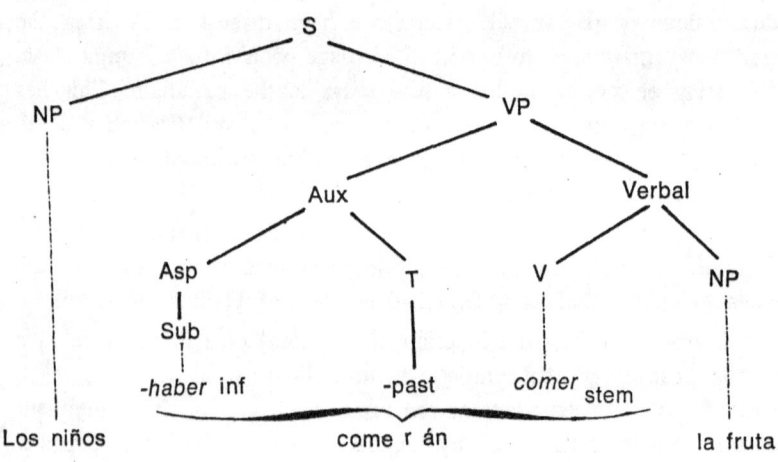

2)

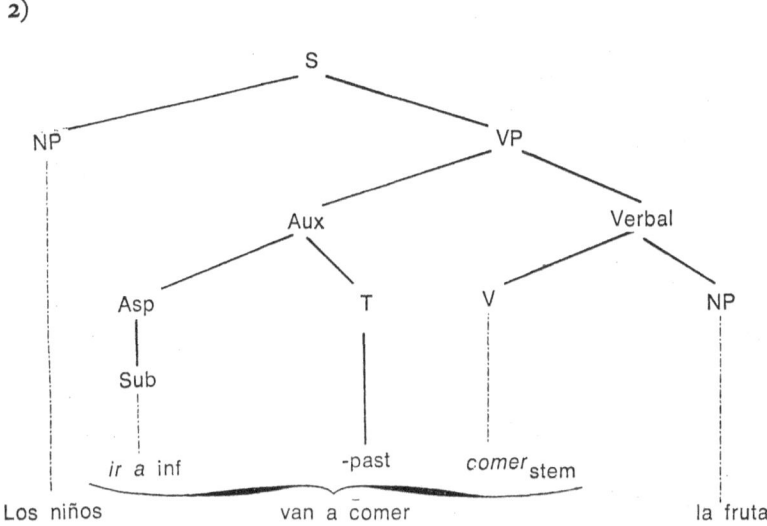

In both cases, two transformational rules apply: 1) verb agreement, which assigns the correct desinence, according to the person and number of the subject; and 2) affix shift, which moves the affixes to the right and attaches them to the first available verb stem (the affix closest to the verb stem is attached first).

The rules given in Dubois — Dubois-Charlier, revised, are the following:

$$
\begin{aligned}
&\text{Aux} \rightarrow \text{T} + (\text{Perf}) + (\text{M}) + (\text{Perf}) \\
&\text{T} \rightarrow \left(\left\{ \begin{array}{c} \text{Future} \\ \text{Subj} \end{array} \right\} \right) + \left\{ \begin{array}{c} \text{Pres} \\ \text{Past} \end{array} \right\} + \text{P} + \text{N} \\
&\text{Future} \rightarrow \left\{ \begin{array}{c} r \\ \text{aller } r \end{array} \right\} \\
&\text{Past} \rightarrow \left\{ \begin{array}{c} \text{imp} \\ \text{pret} \end{array} \right\}
\end{aligned}
$$

This last analysis, as it stands, is unsatisfactory (as it was before my additional rewrite rule) because it allows the future morphemes to be added to the preterit. The authors have noted this and only say that: "... les combinaisons Futur + Imparf et Futur + [préterit] donnent le même résultat (c'est-à-dire le conditionnel)..."[49] This

---

[49] Dubois — Dubois-Charlier 1970, 99.

statement is inadequate because it does not explicitly disallow the combination Futur + préterit. What seems to be required, if the order of the rules as given by the authors is to be retained, is a rule of the type: Past → imp/Fut—, which specifies that Past be written as imperfect in the environment of Future. This rule would be inserted between the rewrite rules for Future and Past. I believe that a more satisfactory solution would be to re-order the authors' rules, but I shall not attempt that here. Note that this problem does not arise in Hadlich's analysis, because the selection of subsequence automatically rules out a choice between perfective and imperfective.

The representation of *Les enfants vont manger des fruits*, using these revised rules, would now be as follows:

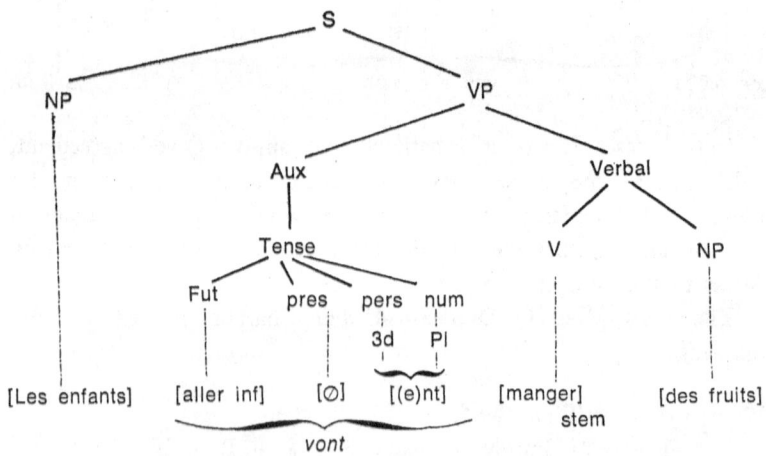

As in Hadlich, a transformational rule would shift the infinitive affix to the right. The person-number affixes, however, require a more complicated rule, stating, in effect, that they are shifted to the right, *unless* there is a verb stem somewhere in the auxiliary component (this would include the modals), in which case they are attached to this stem.

This bipartite division of futurity or subsequence has been suggested for French by Gross.[50] In his discussion, the author states that

---

[50] Gross 1968, 12-15. I have changed Gross' method of notation to the more familiar one used by Hadlich and Dubois — Dubois-Charlier.

verb forms may be decomposed into three parts: stem, tense, person-number affix. Tense (T) is further sub-divided as follows:

$$T \rightarrow \begin{Bmatrix} \text{Pres} \\ \text{Imp} \end{Bmatrix} \text{(fut) (aux)}$$

$$\text{Fut} \rightarrow (\text{r(aller)}) \text{ inf}$$

$$\text{Aux} \rightarrow \begin{Bmatrix} \begin{Bmatrix} \text{r(avoir)} \\ \text{r(être)} \end{Bmatrix} \text{ past participle} \\ \text{r(venir) de infinitive} \end{Bmatrix} \text{[51]}$$

While Gross is correct, I believe, in treating the future in this manner, his analysis is, in general, unsatisfactory. He states at the outset that he excludes from his study a number of tenses no longer used in Spoken French (notably the passé simple), implying that his analysis is based on Spoken French. On the other hand, he does not account for the *formes surcomposées*: "Alors que nous avons exclu divers temps pour la raison qu'ils n'étaient plus employés en français parlé standard, les temps surcomposés semblent être employés par de nombreux locuteurs; néanmoins il ne nous a pas été possible d'obtenir des données solides sur leur utilisation, mis à part le fait qu'ils sont beaucoup plus naturels avec le verbe *finir* qu'avec tout autre verbe." [52] Furthermore, since Gross is interested in single verb forms only, rather than in verbal constructions, he does not include a modal element, which I think Dubois — Dubois-Charlier are correct in using for French.

As in traditional grammar, so also in transformational grammar, we find no unanimous agreement on what makes up the auxiliary component, on how *vado (ad)* plus infinitive should be represented, or, indeed, if it should be represented at all. I have tried to state my belief that, if the facts concerning the use of the construction are to be correctly reflected, not only must *vado (ad)* plus infinitive be represented in the auxiliary component, but it must also be treated at the same level as the markers for the synthetic future.

---

[51] r(aller) indicates the root (*racine*) of *aller*, the verb in parentheses.
[52] Gross 1968, 17.

APPENDIX I

NAMES OF THE INDICATIVE TENSES IN SELECTED SPANISH GRAMMARS [1]

	Real Academia	Seco	Alonso—Henríquez Ureña	Alonso, Martín
amo	presente			
amaba	pretérito imperfecto			
amé	pretérito indefinido		pretérito	pretérito perfecto absoluto
he amado	pretérito perfecto			pretérito perfecto actual
había amado	pretérito pluscuamperfecto			pluscuamperfecto
hube amado	pretérito anterior			
amaré	futuro imperfecto		futuro	futuro absoluto
habré amado	futuro perfecto			futuro compuesto
amaría	simple o [2] imperfecto	futuro potencial simple	[2]	potencial simple [3]
habría amado	compuesto o perfecto [2]	futuro potencial compuesto	[2]	potencial compuesto [3]

[1] Blank spaces indicate that the term used is the same as that in the first column.

[2] Classified not as indicative mode, but rather as modo potencial.

[3] Classified as subjunctives.

Appendix I (*Continued*)

	Criado de Val	*Gili y Gaya*	*Lenz* [4]	*Bello*
amo				
amaba	imperfecto		imperfecto	co-pretérito
amé	pretérito	pretérito perfecto absoluto	pretérito	pretérito
he amado	perfecto	pretérito perfecto actual	perfecto	antepresente
había amado	pluscuamperfecto	pluscuamperfecto	pluscuamperfecto	ante-co-pretérito
hube amado	anterior	antepretérito	pretérito perfecto	ante-pretérito
amaré	futuro simple	futuro absoluto	futuro	futuro
habré amado	futuro compuesto	antefuturo		ante-futuro
amaría	condicional simple	futuro hipotético	pospretérito	pos-pretérito
habría amado	condicional compuesto	antefuturo hipotético	pospretérito perfecto	ante-pospretérito

---

[4] Lenz also adds the pluscuamperfecto perfecto simple (*cantara*), which is archaic (cf. Portuguese); and the futuro hipotético (*cantare*) and futuro hipotético perfecto (*hubiere cantado*), both of which are treated as subjunctives in all other grammars.

Appendix II

NAMES OF THE INDICATIVE TENSES IN SELECTED PORTUGUESE GRAMMARS [1]

	Bechara, Cunha, Victoria, Azevedo Torres, Rocha Lima	Silveira Bueno	Melo
canto	presente		presente do indicativo
cantava	pretérito imperfeito	imperfeito	imperfeito do indicativo
cantei	pretérito perfeito	perfeito	pretérito perfeito do indicativo
cantara	pretérito mais-que-perfeito	mais-que-perfeito	mais-que-perfeito do indicativo
cantarei	futuro do presente	futuro	
cantaria	futuro do pretérito	imperfeito (cond) [3]	
tenho ou hei cantado	pretérito perfeito composto		perfeito do indicativo
tinha ou havia cantado	pretérito mais-que-perfeito composto	mais-que-perfeito composto	mais-que-perfeito do indicativo
terei ou haverei cantado	futuro do presente composto	futuro anterior	
teria ou haveria cantado	futuro do pretérito composto [2]	imperfeito composto (cond) [3]	

[1] Blank spaces indicate that the term used is the same as that in the first column.

[2] Rocha Lima also adds *tivera ou houvera cantado*.

[3] These two forms are listed as conditionals, which Silveira Bueno classifies separately from the indicative.

APPENDIX III

NAMES OF THE INDICATIVE TENSES IN SELECTED FRENCH GRAMMARS [1]

	Chevalier et al.,[2] Gougenheim	Wartburg— Zumthor	Dauzat [3]	Mauger
je chante	présent			
je chantais	imparfait			
je chantai	passé simple	passé défini	préterit	
je chanterai	futur			
je chanterais	conditionnel		présent [4]	présent [4]
j'ai chanté	passé composé	passé indéfini	parfait	
j'avais chanté	plus-que-parfait			
j'eus chanté	passé antérieur			
j'aurai chanté	futur antérieur			
j'aurais chanté	conditionnel passé		imparfait [4]	passé [4]
j'ai eu chanté	passé sur-composé		5	
j'avais eu chanté	plus-que par-fait surcomposé			
j'eus eu chanté	passé antérieur surcomposé			5
j'aurai eu chanté	futur antérieur surcomposé		5	
j'aurais eu chanté	conditionnel passé surcomposé		imparfait [4] surcomposé	

---

[1] Blank spaces indicate that the term used is the same as that in the first column.

[2] Chevalier *et al.* add *je vais chanter* and *j'allais chanter* to the paradigm as futur periphrastique.

[3] Dauzat adds *je vais chanter* as futur proche and *je viens de chanter* as passé proche.

[4] These forms are listed separately under conditionnel.

[5] These forms are not included in the paradigm.

Appendix III (Continued)

	Académie française	LeBidois—LeBidois	Grevisse [6]
je chante			
je chantais			
je chantai			
je chanterai			
je chanterais	présent [4]		futur du passé [7]
j'ai chanté			
j'avais chanté			
j'eus chanté			
j'aurai chanté			
j'aurais chanté	passé [4]		futur antérieur du passé [7]
j'ai eu chanté	5		
j'avais eu chanté	5		
j'eus eu chanté	5		
j'aurai eu chanté	5		
j'aurais eu chanté	5	conditionnel surcomposé	

---

[6] While Grevisse does not add *aller* plus infinitive to the paradigm, he does state: "On range aussi parmi les temps composés ceux qui se forment à l'aide des semi-auxiliaires *aller, devoir*..." (Grevisse 1964, 610).

[7] The author says that these have the same form as conditionals.

BIBLIOGRAPHY

WORKS CITED

Académie française, *Grammaire de l'Académie française* (Paris 1932).
Almeida Tôrres, Artur de, *Moderna gramática expositiva da lingua portuguêsa* (17th ed., Rio de Janeiro 1965).
Alonso, Amado, *Estudios lingüísticos: temas españoles* (Madrid 1954).
Alonso, Amado and Pedro Henríquez Ureña, *Gramática castellana* (16th ed., Buenos Aires 1959).
Alonso, Martín, *Gramática del español contemporáneo* (Madrid 1968).
Antonini, Abbé, *Principes de la grammaire françoise pratique et raisonnée* (Paris 1753).
Azevedo Filho, Leodegário A. de, *Gramática básica da língua portuguêsa* (Rio de Janeiro 1968).
Badía Margarit, Antonio, "Regles d'esquivar vocables o mots grossers o pagesívols." Unas normas del siglo xv sobre pureza de la lengua catalana, *Boletín de la Real Academia de Buenas Letras de Barcelona* 23 (1950), 137-152.
——, *Gramática catalana*, Vol. 1 (Madrid 1962).
Bal, Willy, *Introduction aux études de linguistique romane* (Paris 1966).
Baldinger, Kurt, *La formación de los dominios lingüísticos en la península ibérica* (Madrid 1963).
Bauche, Henri, *Le langage populaire* (2nd ed., Paris 1929).
Bec, Pierre, *La langue occitane* (2nd ed., Paris 1967).
Bechara, Evanildo, *Moderna gramática portuguêsa* (13th ed., São Paulo 1968).
Bello, Andrés, *Gramática de la lengua castellana destinada al uso de los americanos* (Caracas 1972).
Berchem, Theodor, "Considerations sur le parfait périphrastique *vado* + *infinitif* en catalan et gallo-roman, *Actas del XI Congreso Internacional de lingüística y filología románicas*, Vol. 3 (Madrid 1968).
Bjerrome, Gunnar, *Le patois de Bagnes (Valais)* (Stockholm 1957).
Bourciez, Édouard, *Éléments de linguistique romane* (4th ed., Paris 1956).
Buck, Carl D., *Comparative grammar of Greek and Latin* (Chicago 1933).
Bull, William E., *Spanish for teachers: applied linguistics* (New York 1965).
Burt, Marina K., *From deep to surface structure* (New York 1971).
Casas Homs, José María (ed.), *"Torcimany" de Luis de Averço*, Vol. 1 (Barcelona 1956).
Chaurand, Jacques, *Les parlers de la Thiérache et du Laonnois* (Paris 1968).

Chaves de Melo, Gladstone, *Gramática fundamental da língua portuguêsa* (Rio de Janeiro 1968).
Chevalier, Jean Claude et al., *Grammaire Larousse du français contemporain* (Paris 1964).
Chomsky, Noam, *Aspects of the theory of syntax* (Cambridge, Mass. 1965).
Colón, Germán, Le parfait périphrastique catalan "va + infinitif," *Boletim de Filologia* 18 (1959), 165-176.
Criado de Val, Manuel, *Gramática española* (3rd ed., Madrid 1966).
Cuervo, Rufino José, *Diccionario de construcción y régimen de la lengua castellana* (Paris 1886-93).
Cunha, Celso, *Gramática do português contemporâneo* (Belo Horizonte, Brazil 1970).
Damourette, Jacques and Édouard Pichon, *Essai de grammaire de la langue française*, Vol. 5 (Paris 1936).
Dauzat, Albert, *Grammaire raisonnée de la langue française* (4th ed., Paris 1958).
Dubois, Jean and Françoise Dubois-Charlier, *Éléments de linguistique française: syntaxe* (Paris 1970).
Elcock, William Dennis, *The Romance languages* (London 1960).
Entwistle, William J., *The Spanish language, together with Portuguese, Catalan and Basque* (2nd ed., London 1962).
Ernout, Alfred, *Morphologie historique du latin* (Paris 1945).
Ernout, Alfred and François Thomas, *Syntaxe latine* (2nd ed., Paris 1953).
Espinosa, Aurelio M., *Cuentos populares españoles* (Madrid 1946).
García de Diego, Vicente, *Manual de dialectología española* (2nd ed., Madrid 1959).
Gatien-Arnoult, Adolphe (ed.), *Monumens de la littérature romane*, Vol. 3 (Toulouse 1843).
Gili y Gaya, Samuel, *Curso superior de sintaxis española* (7th ed., Barcelona 1960).
Gougenheim, Georges, *Étude sur les périphrases verbales de la langue française* (Paris 1929).
———, *Système grammatical de la langue française* (Paris 1938).
———, *Grammaire de la langue française du seizième siècle* (Lyon 1951).
Grandgent, Charles H., *An introduction to Vulgar Latin* (Boston 1934; reprinted by Hafner Publishing Co., New York 1962).
Grevisse, Maurice, *Le bon usage* (8th ed., Gembloux and Paris 1964).
Grimes, Larry, Sintaxis de "futuridad" en dos representaciones del habla popular mexicano, *Archiv für das Studium der neueren Sprachen und Literaturen* 204 (1967-68) 349-352.
Gross, Maurice, *Grammaire transformationelle du français: syntaxe du verbe* (Paris 1968).
Hadlich, Roger L., *A transformational grammar of Spanish* (Englewood Cliffs, N. J. 1971).
Haensch, Günther, *Las hablas de la Alta Ribagorza (Pirineo aragonés)* (Zaragoza 1960).
Hall, Robert A., Jr., *Haitian Creole: grammar, texts, vocabulary* (Philadelphia 1953).
Henrichsen, Arne-Johan, La périphrase *anar* + infinitif en ancien occitan, *Omagiu... Rosetti* (Bucharest 1966) 357-363.

Hunnius, Klaus, Der verbale Ausdruck der Zukunft in spanischen Volksmärchen, *Archiv für das Studium der neueren Sprachen und Literaturen* 204 (1967-68) 342-345.
Imbs, Paul, *L'Emploi des temps verbaux en français moderne* (Paris 1960).
Jacobs, Roderick A. and Peter S. Rosenbaum, *English transformational grammar* (Waltham, Mass. 1968).
Jahncke, Isolde, *L'Expression du futur en portugais, galicien et "brésilien"* (Dissertation, École Pratique des Hautes Études 1966).
Jordana, C.A., *El català i el castellà comparats* (Barcelona 1968).
Juilland, Alphonse and Marilyn J. Conwell, *Louisiana French grammar* (The Hague 1963).
Juilland, Alphonse and Eugenio Chang-Rodríguez, *Frequency dictionary of Spanish words* (The Hague 1964).
Juilland, Alphonse et al., *Frequency dictionary of French words* (The Hague 1970).
Kahane, Henry and Harriet Hutter, The verbal categories of colloquial Brazilian Portuguese, *Word* 9 (1953) 16-44.
Kany, Charles Emil, *American-Spanish syntax* (2nd ed., Chicago 1951).
Keniston, Hayward, *Spanish syntax list* (New York 1937).
Kent, Roland G., *The forms of Latin* (Baltimore 1946).
Lancelot, Claude and Antoine Arnauld, *Grammaire générale et raisonnée* (Paris 1660).
Lanly, André, *Le français d'Afrique du Nord* (Paris 1970).
Lanusse, Maxime, *De l'influence du dialecte gascon sur la langue française* (Paris 1893).
Lenz, Rodolfo, *La oración y sus partes* (2nd ed., Madrid 1925).
LeBidois, Georges and Robert LeBidois, *Syntaxe du français moderne*, 2 Vols. (2nd ed., Paris 1967).
Lerch, Eugen, *Die Verwendung des romanischen Futurums als Ausdruck eines sittlichen Sollens* (Leipzig 1919).
Liles, Bruce L., *An introductory transformational grammar* (Englewood Cliffs, N.J. 1971).
Lope Blanch, Juan M., *Observaciones sobre la sintaxis del español hablado en México* (México 1953).
Lyons, John, *Introduction to theoretical linguistics* (Cambridge 1969).
Marquèze-Pouey, L., L'auxiliaire aller dans l'expression du passé en gascon, *Via Domitia* 2 (1955) 111-121.
Martinet, André, L'économie des formes du verbe en français parlé, *Studia... L. Spitzer* (Bern 1958) 309-326.
Massignon, Geneviève, *Les parlers français d'Acadie*, 2 Vols. (Paris 1962).
Mattoso Camara, Joaquim, Jr., *The Portuguese language* (Chicago 1972).
Mauger, Gaston, *Grammaire pratique du français d'aujourd'hui* (Paris 1968).
Maupas, Charles, *Grammaire et syntaxe françoise* (Paris 1625).
Menéndez Pidal, Ramón, *Cantar de mío Cid, texto, gramática y vocabulario*, Vol. 1 (Madrid 1954).
Migliorini, Bruno, *Storia della lingua italiana* (Firenze 1966).
Moll, Francesc de B., *Gramàtica catalana* (Palma de Mallorca 1968).
Montes, José Joaquín, Sobre la categoría de futuro en el español de Colombia, *Boletín del Instituto Caro y Cuervo* 17 (1962) 527-555.
Müller, Bodo, Das lateinische Futurum und die romanischen Ausdrucksweisen für das Futurische geschehen, *Romanische Forschungen* 76 (1964) 44-97.

Padrón, Alfredo F., Giros sintácticos usados en Cuba, *Boletín del Instituto Caro y Cuervo* 5 (1950) 163-175.
Palmer, Leonard Robert, *The Latin language* (London 1954).
Pohl, Jacques, A propos de "vouloir," auxiliaire du futur, *Le Français Moderne* 29 (1961) 62-64.
Pompilus, Pradel, *La langue française en Haïti* (Paris 1961).
Pulgram, Ernst, Synthetic and analytic morphological constructs, *Festschrift Alwin Kuhn = Innsbrucker Beiträge zur Kulturwissenschaft* 9/10 (1963) 35-42.
———, Trends and predictions, *To Honor Roman Jakobson*, Vol. 2 (The Hague 1967) 1634-1649.
Raillet, Philippus, *Triumphus linguae gallicae* (Lyon 1654).
Real Academia Española, *Gramática de la lengua española* (Madrid 1959).
Regnier-Desmarais, Abbé, *Traité de la grammaire françoise* (Paris 1705).
Rocha Lima, Carlos Henrique da, *Gramática normativa da língua portuguêsa* (15th ed., Rio de Janeiro 1972).
Rohlfs, Gerhard, Das romanische *habeo*-Futurum und Konditionalis, *Archivum Romanicum* 6 (1922) 105-154.
———, *Historische Grammatik der italienischen Sprache*, Vol. 2 (Bern 1949).
———, *Diferenciación léxica de las lenguas románicas* (Madrid 1960).
———, *Le gascon* (2nd ed., Tübingen 1970).
Ronjat, Jules, *Grammaire istorique [sic] des parlers provençaux modernes*, Vol. 3 (Montpellier 1937).
Sáez-Godoy, Leopoldo, La expresión verbal de lo futuro (del XVII al siglo XX), *Archiv für das Studium der neueren Sprachen und Literaturen* 204 (1967-68) 334-341.
Schiby, Baruch, Notes sur les juifs de Thessalonique, *Actas del primer simposio de estudios sefardíes* (Madrid 1970) 91-94.
Seco, Rafael, *Manual de gramática española* (9th ed., Madrid 1968).
Silva Dias, Augusto Epifânio da, *Syntaxe historica portuguêsa* (Lisbon 1959).
Silveira Bueno, Francisco da, *Gramática normativa da língua portuguêsa* (5th ed., São Paulo 1958).
Simon, W., Charakteristik des judenspanischen Dialekts von Saloniki, *Zeitschrift für romanische Philologie* 40 (1920) 655-689.
Sjögren, Håkan, *Zum Gebrauch des Futurs im Altlatein* (Uppsala 1906).
Stockwell, Robert P. et al., *The grammatical structures of English and Spanish* (Chicago 1965).
Tagliavini, Carlo, *Le origini delle lingue neolatine* (5th ed., Bologna 1969).
Teyssier, Paul, *La langue de Gil Vicente* (Paris 1959).
Thielmann, Philipp, 'Habere' mit dem Infinitiv und die Entstehung des romanischen Futurums, *Archiv für lateinische Lexicographie und Grammatik* 2 (1885) 48-89, 157-202.
Thogmartin, Clyde O., Jr., *The French dialect of Old Mines, Missouri* (Dissertation, University of Michigan 1970).
Thomas, Earl, Emerging patterns of the Brazilian language, in Eric N. Baklanoff (ed.), *New perspectives of Brazil* (Nashville 1966) 264-297.
Tiktin, Hariton, Die rumänische Sprache, in Gustav Gröber (ed.), *Grundriss der romanischen Philologie*, Vol. 1 (2nd ed., Strasbourg 1905).
Väänänen, Veikko, *Introduction au latin vulgaire* (2nd ed., Paris 1967).
Valesio, Paolo, The Romance synthetic future pattern and its first attestations, *Lingua* 20 (1968) 113-161, 279-307.
———, La genesi del futuro romanzo, *Lingua e Stile* 4 (1969) 405-412.

Victoria, Luis A. P., *Gramática brasileira da língua portuguêsa* (Rio de Janeiro 1968).
Vidos, Benedik Elemer, *Manual de lingüística románica* (Madrid 1963).
Wagner, Max Leopold, Flessione nominale e verbale del sardo antico e moderno, *L'Italia Dialettale* 14, 15 (1938-39) 93-170, 1-29.
Wartburg, Walther von, *Évolution et structure de la langue française* (7th ed., Bern 1965).
Wartburg, Walther von and Paul Zumthor, *Précis de syntaxe du français contemporain* (Bern 1958).
Wolfe, David E., *A generative-transformational analysis of Spanish verb forms* (Dissertation, University of Michigan 1966).
Woodcock, Eric Charles, *A new Latin syntax* (Cambridge, Mass. 1958).
Zamora Vicente, Alonso, *Dialectología española* (Madrid 1967).

ABBREVIATIONS AND TEXTS CITED

Caes., B. G.	Gaius Julius Caesar, *Commentarii de bello gallico*, ed. by Gianni Gervasoni (2nd ed., Milan 1951).
Celestina	Fernando Rojas, *La Celestina*, ed. by Julio Cejador y Frauca, 2 Vols. (Madrid 1968).
Cervantes	Cervantes Saavedra, Miguel de, *Obras completas*, 7 Vols. (Madrid 1917-23).
Chanson de Roland	*La chanson de Roland*, ed. by Joseph Bédier (Paris 1939).
Cic.	Marcus Tullius Cicero.
Epist. ad fam.	*Epistulae ad familiares*, in *Cicero: The letters to his friends*, ed. by W. Glynn Williams, Vol. 1 (London 1927).
Pro Sexto	*Oratio pro Sexto Roscio Amerino*, in *Cicero: The speeches*, ed. by John Henry Freese (London 1930).
Diàlegs	Sant Gregori, *Diàlegs*, ed. by Mn. Jaume Bofarull (Barcelona 1931).
Dialogues of Saint Gregory	*Gregorii Magni Dialogi Libri IV*, ed. by Umberto Moricca (Rome 1924).
Fredegar, *Chron.*	Fredegarii Scholastici *Chronicum*, in Migne, Vol. 71 (Paris 1846) 608-703.
Góngora	Luis de Góngora y Argote, *Obras completas*, ed. by Juan Millé y Giménez e Isabel Millé y Giménez (Madrid 1961).
Grant cronica	Juan Fernández de Heredia, *Grant cronica de Espanya Libros I-II*, ed. by Regina Af Geijerstam (Uppsala 1964).

Greg., *Lib. uit. pat.*	Gregorius, *Liber uitae patrum*, in Migne, Vol. 71 (Paris 1858) 1009-1096.
Il Raguet	in Francesco Scipione Maffei, *Opere drammatiche e poesie varie* (Bari 1928) 165-224.
La vida de Santa María Egipciaca	*La vida de Santa María Egipciaca*, ed. by María S. de Andrés Castellanos (Madrid 1964).
Livy, *A. U. C.*	*Titi Livi Ab urbe condita*, ed. by Robert S. Conway and Carol Walters (Oxford 1914-29).
Lope	Lope Félix de Vega Carpio, *Comedias*, ed. by J. Gómez Ocerín and R. M. Tenreiro (Madrid 1960).
Melusine (Brunet)	Jehan d'Arras, *Melusine*, ed. by Charles Brunet (Paris 1854).
Melusine (Stouff)	Jean d'Arras, *Melusine*, ed. by Louis Stouff (Paris 1932).
Migne	Migne, Jacques Paul, *Patrologia cursus completus*, 221 Vols. (Paris 1844-64).
Miracles	*Miracles de Nostre Dame par personnages, publiés d'après le manuscrit de la Bibliothèque Nationale* (Paris 1876-93).
Moralité	*Moralité ou histoire rommaine*, in *Ancien Théatre françois*, ed. by Emmanuel le Duc, Vol. 3 (Paris 1854).
Mystères	*Mystères provençaux du quinzième siècle*, ed. by Alfred Jeanroy and Henri Teulié (Toulouse 1893).
Os Lusíadas	Luis de Camões, *Os Lusíadas*, ed. by Francisco da Silveira Bueno (São Paulo 1960).
Pantagruel	in Rabelais, François, *Le quart livre*, ed. by Robert Marichal (Geneva 1947).
Perceval	Robert de Borron, *Perceval ou la quête du Saint Graal*, in *Le Saint-Graal*, ed. by Eugène Hucher, Vol. 1 (Mans 1875).
Per.	*Itinerarium Egeriae (Peregrinatio Aetheriae)*, ed. by Otto Prinz (Heidelberg 1960).
Petr.	Pétrone, *Le satiricon*, ed. by Alfred Ernout (3rd ed., Paris 1950).
Philomena	*Gesta Karoli Magni ad Carcassonam et Narbonam*, ed. by Friedrich Eduard Schneegans (Halle 1898).

BIBLIOGRAPHY

Plaut.	*T. Macci Plauti Comoediae*, ed. by Wallace M. Lindsay (Oxford 1903).
Bac.	*Bacchides*, Vol. 1.
Cas.	*Casina*, Vol. 1.
Most.	*Mostellaria*, Vol. 2.
Pseud.	*Pseudolus*, Vol. 2.
Poema de mío Cid	*Poema de mío Cid*, ed. by Ramón Menéndez Pidal (Madrid 1960).
Primera crónica general de España	*Primera crónica general de España*, ed. by Ramón Menéndez Pidal, 2 Vols. (Madrid 1955).
Sal., *Vitae patrum*	Salonius, Arne Henrik, *Vitae Patrum; kritische Untersuchung über Text, Syntax und Wortschatz der spätlateinische Vitae Patrum* (Lund 1920).
Tert., *De Res.*	Tertulliani Presbyteri carthaginensis, *Liber de resurrectione carnis*, in Migne, Vol. 2 (Paris 1844) 791-886.
Verg., *Aen.*	Publius Vergilius Maro, *The Aeneid*, ed. by J. W. Mackail (Oxford 1930).

NORTH CAROLINA STUDIES IN THE ROMANCE LANGUAGES AND LITERATURES

I.S.B.N. Prefix 0-8078-

Recent Titles

THE LEGEND OF THE "SIETE INFANTES DE LARA" (*Refundición toledana de la crónica de 1344* versión), study and edition by Thomas A. Lathrop. 1972. (No. 122). -922-7.

STRUCTURE AND IDEOLOGY IN BOIARDO'S "ORLANDO INNAMORATO," by Andrea di Tommaso. 1972. (No. 123). -923-5.

STUDIES IN HONOR OF ALFRED G. ENGSTROM, edited by Robert T. Cargo and Emmanuel J. Mickel, Jr. 1972. (No. 124). -924-3.

A CRITICAL EDITION WITH INTRODUCTION AND NOTES OF GIL VICENTE'S "FLORESTA DE ENGANOS," by Constantine Christopher Stathatos. 1972. (No. 125). -925-1.

LI ROMANS DE WITASSE LE MOINE. *Roman du treizième siècle*. Édité d'après le manuscrit, fonds français 1553, de la Bibliothèque Nationale, Paris, par Denis Joseph Conlon. 1972. (No. 126). -926-X.

EL CRONISTA PEDRO DE ESCAVIAS. *Una vida del Siglo XV*, por Juan Bautista Avalle-Arce. 1972. (No. 127). -927-8.

AN EDITION OF THE FIRST ITALIAN TRANSLATION OF THE "CELESTINA," by Kathleen V. Kish. 1973. (No. 128). -928-6.

MOLIÈRE MOCKED. THREE CONTEMPORARY HOSTILE COMEDIES: *Zélinde, Le portrait du peintre, Elomire Hypocondre*, by Frederick Wright Vogler. 1973. (No. 129). -929-4.

C.-A. SAINTE-BEUVE. *Chateaubriand et son groupe littéraire sous l'empire.* Index alphabétique et analytique établi par Lorin A. Uffenbeck. 1973. (No 130). -930-8.

THE ORIGINS OF THE BAROQUE CONCEPT OF "PEREGRINATIO," by Juergen Hahn. 1973. (No. 131). -931-6.

THE "AUTO SACRAMENTAL" AND THE PARABLE IN SPANISH GOLDEN AGE LITERATURE, by Donald Thaddeus Dietz. 1973. (No. 132). -932-4.

FRANCISCO DE OSUNA AND THE SPIRIT OF THE LETTER, by Laura Calvert. 1973. (No. 133). -933-2.

ITINERARIO DI AMORE: DIALETTICA DI AMORE E MORTE NELLA VITA NUOVA, by Margherita de Bonfils Templer. 1973. (No. 134). -934-0.

L'IMAGINATION POETIQUE CHEZ DU BARTAS: ELEMENTS DE SENSIBILITE BAROQUE DANS LA "CREATION DU MONDE," by Bruno Braunrot. 1973. (No. 135). -934-0.

ARTUS DESIRE: PRIEST AND PAMPHLETEER OF THE SIXTEENTH CENTURY, by Frank S. Giese. 1973. (No. 136). -936-7.

JARDIN DE NOBLES DONZELLAS, FRAY MARTIN DE CORDOBA, by Harriet Goldberg. 1974. (No. 137). -937-5.

MYTHE ET PSYCHOLOGIE CHEZ MARIE DE FRANCE DANS "GUIGEMAR", par Antoinette Knapton. 1975. (No. 142). -942-1.

THE LYRIC POEMS OF JEHAN FROISSART: A CRITICAL EDITION, by Rob Roy McGregor, Jr. 1975. (No. 143). -943-X.

THE HISPANO-PORTUGUESE CANCIONERO OF THE HISPANIC SOCIETY OF AMERICA, by Arthur Askins. 1974. (No. 144). -944-8.

HISTORIA Y BIBLIOGRAFÍA DE LA CRÍTICA SOBRE EL "POEMA DE MÍO CID" (1750-1971), por Miguel Magnotta. 1976. (No. 145). -945-6.

LES ENCHANTEMENZ DE BRETAIGNE. AN EXTRACT FROM A THIRTEENTH CENTURY PROSE ROMANCE "LA SUITE DU MERLIN", edited by Patrick C. Smith. 1977. (No. 146). -9146-0.

When ordering please cite the *ISBN Prefix* plus the last four digits for each title.

Send orders to: University of North Carolina Press
Chapel Hill
North Carolina 27514
U. S. A.

NORTH CAROLINA STUDIES IN THE ROMANCE LANGUAGES AND LITERATURES

I.S.B.N. Prefix 0-8078-

Recent Titles

THE DRAMATIC WORKS OF ÁLVARO CUBILLO DE ARAGÓN, by Shirley B. Whitaker. 1975. (No. 149). -949-9.
A CONCORDANCE TO THE "ROMAN DE LA ROSE" OF GUILLAUME DE LORRIS, by Joseph R. Danos. 1976. (No. 156). 0-88438-403-9.
POETRY AND ANTIPOETRY: A STUDY OF SELECTED ASPECTS OF MAX JACOB'S POETIC STYLE, by Annette Thau. 1976. (No. 158). -005-X.
FRANCIS PETRARCH, SIX CENTURIES LATER, by Aldo Scaglione. 1975. (No. 159).
STYLE AND STRUCTURE IN GRACIÁN'S "EL CRITICÓN", by Marcia L. Welles, 1976. (No. 160). -007-6.
MOLIERE: TRADITIONS IN CRITICISM, by Laurence Romero. 1974 (Essays, No. 1). -001-7.
CHRÉTIEN'S JEWISH GRAIL. A NEW INVESTIGATION OF THE IMAGERY AND SIGNIFICANCE OF CHRÉTIEN DE TROYES'S GRAIL EPISODE BASED UPON MEDIEVAL HEBRAIC SOURCES, by Eugene J. Weinraub. 1976. (Essays, No. 2). -002-5.
STUDIES IN TIRSO, I, by Ruth Lee Kennedy. 1974. (Essays, No. 3). -003-3.
VOLTAIRE AND THE FRENCH ACADEMY, by Karlis Racevskis. 1975. (Essays, No. 4). -004-1.
THE NOVELS OF MME RICCOBONI, by Joan Hinde Stewart. 1976. (Essays, No. 8). -008-4.
FIRE AND ICE: THE POETRY OF XAVIER VILLAURRUTIA, by Merlin H. Forster. 1976. (Essays, No. 11). -011-4.
THE THEATER OF ARTHUR ADAMOV, by John J. McCann. 1975. (Essays, No. 13). -013-0.
AN ANATOMY OF POESIS: THE PROSE POEMS OF STÉPHANE MALLARMÉ, by Ursula Franklin. 1976. (Essays, No. 16). -016-5.
LAS MEMORIAS DE GONZALO FERNÁNDEZ DE OVIEDO, Vols. I and II, by Juan Bautista Avalle-Arce. 1974. (Texts, Textual Studies, and Translations, Nos. 1 and 2). -401-2; 402-0.
GIACOMO LEOPARDI: THE WAR OF THE MICE AND THE CRABS, translated, introduced and annotated by Ernesto G. Caserta. 1976. (Texts, Textual Studies, and Translations, No. 4). -404-7.
LUIS VÉLEZ DE GUEVARA: A CRITICAL BIBLIOGRAPHY, by Mary G. Hauer. 1975. (Texts, Textual Studies, and Translations, No. 5). -405-5.
UN TRÍPTICO DEL PERÚ VIRREINAL: "EL VIRREY AMAT, EL MARQUÉS DE SOTO FLORIDO Y LA PERRICHOLI". EL "DRAMA DE DOS PALANGANAS" Y SU CIRCUNSTANCIA. estudio preliminar, reedición y notas por Guillermo Lohmann Villena. 1976. (Texts, Textual Studies, and Translation, No. 15). -415-2.
LOS NARRADORES HISPANOAMERICANOS DE HOY, edited by Juan Bautista Avalle-Arce. 1973. (Symposia, No. 1). -951-0.
ESTUDIOS DE LITERATURA HISPANOAMERICANA EN HONOR A JOSÉ J. ARROM, edited by Andrew P. Debicki and Enrique Pupo-Walker. 1975. (Symposia, No. 2). -952-9.
MEDIEVAL MANUSCRIPTS AND TEXTUAL CRITICISM, edited by Christopher Kleinhenz. 1976. (Symposia, No. 4). -954-5.
SAMUEL BECKETT. THE ART OF RHETORIC. edited by Edouard Morot-Sir, Howard Harper, and Dougald McMillan III. 1976. (Symposia, No. 5). -955-3.
DELIE. CONCORDANCE, by Jerry Nash. 1976. 2 Volumes. (No. 174).
FIGURES OF REPETITION IN THE OLD PROVENÇAL LYRIC: A STUDY IN THE STYLE OF THE TROUBADOURS, by Nathaniel B. Smith. 1976. (No. 176). -9176-2.

When ordering please cite the *ISBN Prefix* plus the last four digits for each title.

Send orders to: University of North Carolina Press
North Carolina 27514
Chapel Hill
U S. A.

NORTH CAROLINA STUDIES IN THE ROMANCE LANGUAGES AND LITERATURES

I.S.B.N. Prefix 0-8078-

Recent Titles

A CRITICAL EDITION OF LE REGIME TRESUTILE ET TRESPROUFITABLE POUR CONSERVER ET GARDER LA SANTE DU CORPS HUMAIN, by Patricia Willett Cummins. 1977. (No. 177).

THE DRAMA OF SELF IN GUILLAUME APOLLINAIRE'S "ALCOOLS", by Richard Howard Stamelman. 1976. (No. 178). -9178-9.

A CRITICAL EDITION OF "LA PASSION NOSTRE SEIGNEUR" FROM MANUSCRIPT 1131 FROM THE BIBLIOTHEQUE SAINTE-GENEVIEVE, PARIS, by Edward J. Gallagher. 1976. (No. 179). -9179-7.

A QUANTITATIVE AND COMPARATIVE STUDY OF THE VOCALISM OF THE LATIN INSCRIPTIONS OF NORTH AFRICA, BRITAIN, DALMATIA, AND THE BALKANS, by Stephen William Omeltchenko. 1977. (No. 180). -9180-0.

OCTAVIEN DE SAINT-GELAIS "LE SEJOUR D'HONNEUR", edited by Joseph A. James. 1977. (No. 181). -9181-9.

A STUDY OF NOMINAL INFLECTION IN LATIN INSCRIPTIONS, by Paul A. Gaeng. 1977. (No. 182). -9182-7.

THE LIFE AND WORKS OF LUIS CARLOS LÓPEZ, by Martha S. Bazik. 1977. (No. 183). -9183-5.

"THE CORT D'AMOR". A THIRTEENTH-CENTURY ALLEGORICAL ART OF LOVE, by Lowanne E. Jones. 1977. (No. 185). -9185-1.

PHYTONYMIC DERIVATIONAL SYSTEMS IN THE ROMANCE LANGUAGES: STUDIES IN THEIR ORIGIN AND DEVELOPMENT, by Walter E. Geiger. 1978. (No. 187). -9187-8.

LANGUAGE IN GIOVANNI VERGA'S EARLY NOVELS, by Nicholas Patruno. 1977. (No. 188). -9188-6.

BLAS DE OTERO EN SU POESÍA, by Moraima de Semprún Donahue. 1977. (No. 189). -9189-4.

LA ANATOMÍA DE "EL DIABLO COJUELO": DESLINDES DEL GÉNERO ANATOMÍSTICO, por C. George Peale. 1977. (No. 191). -9191-6.

RICHARD SANS PEUR, EDITED FROM "LE ROMANT DE RICHART" AND FROM GILLES CORROZET'S "RICHART SANS PAOUR", by Denis Joseph Conlon. 1977. (No. 192). -9192-4.

MARCEL PROUST'S GRASSET PROOFS. *Commentary and Variants*, by Douglas Alden. 1978. (No. 193). -9193-2.

MONTAIGNE AND FEMINISM, by Cecile Insdorf. 1977. (No. 194). -9194-0.

SANTIAGO F. PUGLIA, AN EARLY PHILADELPHIA PROPAGANDIST FOR SPANISH AMERICAN INDEPENDENCE, by Merle S. Simmons. 1977. (No. 195). -9195-9.

BAROQUE FICTION-MAKING. A STUDY OF GOMBERVILLE'S "POLEXANDRE", by Edward Baron Turk. 1978. (No. 196). -9196-7.

THE TRAGIC FALL: DON ÁLVARO DE LUNA AND OTHER FAVORITES IN SPANISH GOLDEN AGE DRAMA, by Raymond R. MacCurdy. 1978. (No. 197). -9197-5.

A BAHIAN HERITAGE. An Ethnolinguistic Study of African Influences on Bahian Portuguese, by William W. Megenney. 1978. (No. 198). -9198-3.

"LA QUERELLE DE LA ROSE: Letters and Documents", by Joseph L. Baird and John R. Kane. 1978. (No. 199). -9199-1.

TWO AGAINST TIME. *A Study of the very present worlds of Paul Claudel and Charles Péguy*, by Joy Nachod Humes. 1978. (No. 200). -9200-9.

TECHNIQUES OF IRONY IN ANATOLE FRANCE. Essay on *Les sept femmes de la Barbe-Bleue*, by Diane Wolfe Levy. 1978. (No. 201). -9201-7.

THE PERIPHRASTIC FUTURES FORMED BY THE ROMANCE REFLEXES OF "VADO (AD)" "PLUS INFINITIVE, by James Joseph Champion. 1978 (No. 202). -9202-5.

When ordering please cite the *ISBN Prefix* plus the last four digits for each title.

Send orders to: University of North Carolina Press
  Chapel Hill
  North Carolina 27514
  U. S. A.

The Department of Romance Studies Digital Arts and Collaboration Lab at the University of North Carolina at Chapel Hill is proud to support the digitization of the North Carolina Studies in the Romance Languages and Literatures series.

www.ingramcontent.com/pod-product-compliance
Lightning Source LLC
Chambersburg PA
CBHW020422230426
43663CB00007BA/1273